Soul Weaving

Exploring the Tapestry of our Incarnations

By Penelope Genter and others

JOEF Publications

An Imprint of Journey of Enlightenment Foundations

P. O. Box 21603

Sedona, AZ 86341

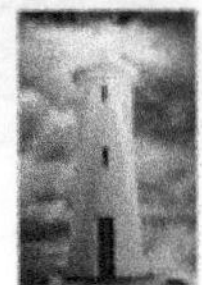

ISBN-13: 978-1721686254

ISBN-10: 1721686258

I have been told that I have been a "fly on the wall" at significant times in history so that I can tell the tale...

I am profoundly grateful for all the soul sisters and brothers that have come together to share their insights and wisdom in order to make this book possible, especially Dr. Jewels Maloney and Rev. Jami Martin for their contributions and help in editing the material. They are able to see things I cannot.

Contents

Soul Weaving - Exploring the Tapestry of our Incarnations

By Penelope Genter and others

Reincarnation... Soul Mates... Soul Groups – what do they mean, and how are we a product of all the lives we have lived? Over half of the world's population believes in reincarnation but how many really understand the importance of it in the lives we are experiencing today?

Penelope is the archetype of the weaver and Penelope Genter embodies this along with many of her soul mates who are conscious channels with past-life recall. They share their remembrance of times past and how the tapestry of experience reveals patterns and lessons of intersecting lives to create a greater understanding of the soul's purpose and our divine dance together.

A unique glimpse behind the veil of existence, Penelope shares her past lives as "a fly on the wall at significant times in history so that she could "tell the tale" and weaves together lessons and experiences into a tapestry of souls. What do Cleopatra, Knights Templar, Joan of Arc, Anne Boleyn and the Impressionists have in common and why have they come back to weave together the fabric of life today? What tools can you use to begin to unravel your own soul's journey? It is a journey down a rabbit hole few have taken, but well worth the trip.

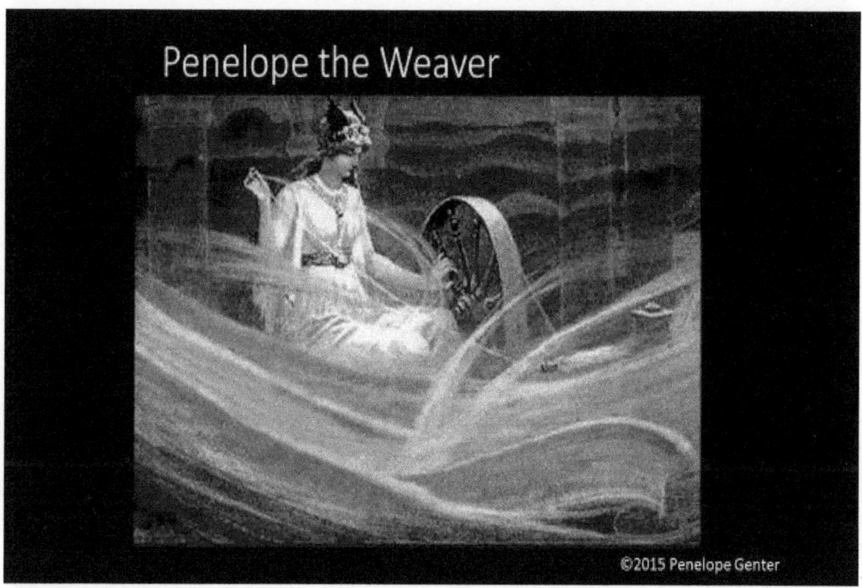

Penelope the Weaver

Penelope is the archetype of the Weaver and that certainly seems to be the theme I chose before entering this incarnation. I was in my fifties before I became aware of the process, as the threads of my life and my experiences began to come together in recognizable patterns that I was able to follow: a breadcrumb trail through the veil to their genesis. It has been said that we see through a glass darkly, but slowly, I began to find clear patches where the illumination of pattern began to shine through.

I was told early-on that I had been a "fly on the wall" at many significant times in history so that I could tell the tale but was not sure what that meant, so I continued through the maze without a clue as to how all the pieces fit together. Little by little I was given snippets of previous lifetimes and who I was then. It is only in the perspective of advanced age that I am able to see how these earlier incarnations prepared me for and gave me the threads I am weaving into the tapestry of today.

This time around I am a Gemini, ruled by the planet Mercury, the planet of communication. My energy center is the fifth or throat chakra. I am a communicator – I write; I speak but more importantly, I listen. I take it all in and then begin to weave thoughts, ideas, and passions into patterns and processes. I guess that what the archetype of Penelope is all about.

Akashic Records and Cellular Memory

- In theosophy and anthroposophy, the **Akashic records** are a compendium of all human events, thoughts, words, emotions, and intent ever to have occurred in the past, present, or future. They are believed by theosophists to be encoded in a non-physical plane of existence known as the etheric plane.

- There is coding in the DNA that contains Akashic records as well as physical characteristics and knowledge.
- It is not unusual for there to be a physical resemblance of a soul from lifetime to lifetime.
- There is frequently a common theme or profession and knowledge that is explored from lifetime to lifetime in different ways.
- Prodigies and savants carry knowledge from previous lifetimes longing for expression.

Reincarnation

- It is the recycling of souls until perfection of the spirit is achieved and reunification with the God spirit occurs.
- This requires that lives be lived in many forms and realms to fill out the dance card of experience.
- You may have some lifetimes as an aspect of gender on both sides of the pole.
- You may have different experiences in different cultures or universes.
- You may have parallel lives, or you may be present in different personalities on this planet in the same lifetime or time period.

Reincarnation and the Church

- The intellectual center of the Roman Empire after the time of Jesus was in Alexandria, Egypt. These groups all taught a form of Christianity that included the doctrine of reincarnation.
- The pro-reincarnation teachings of Plato and Socrates were planted in the Holy Land with the spread of the Greek Language.
- The concept of reincarnation did not mesh with the Roman Empire's political needs.
- In denying the soul's divine origin, the Council of Nicaea in AD 325 implicitly ruled out all possibility of pre-existence and reincarnation, while emphasizing the power and authority of the church over individuals. Early texts supporting the concept of reincarnation were discarded and destroyed by the Council of Nicaea.
- According to data released last year by the Pew Forum on Religion and Public Life, a quarter of Americans now believe in reincarnation.
- Over half of the world population believes in reincarnation.

"The soul returns to earth in a body similar to its last one and has similar talents and inclinations." **– Plato**

Reincarnation and Jesus

New Testament scriptures seem to support that Jesus believed in reincarnation.

"*This is the one ... there has not risen anyone greater than John the Baptist.... And if you are willing to accept it, he is the Elijah who was to come. He who has ears, let him hear.*" *(Matthew 11:11-15)*.

Likewise, in John 3:3 Jesus said, "*I tell you the truth, no one can see the kingdom of God unless he is born again.*"

Belief in reincarnation was part of the gnosis of Egypt and Israel at the time of Jesus.

The intellectual center of the Roman Empire after the crucifixion was in Alexandria, Egypt. These groups all taught a form of Christianity that included the doctrine of reincarnation.

Paramhansa Yogananda on Karma and Immorality

Paramhansa Yogananda came to the United States from India in 1920, bringing to the West the teachings and techniques of yoga, the ancient science of soul awakening. He was the first Master of Yoga to make his home in the West, and his ***Autobiography of a Yogi*** has become the bestselling autobiography of all time, awakening fascination in Westerners with the spiritual teachings of the East.

Yoga is the ancient science of redirecting one's energies inward to produce spiritual awakening. In addition to bringing Americans the most practical and effective techniques of meditation, he showed how these principles can be applied to all areas of life.

Karma

> *"If you sow evil, you will reap evil in the form of suffering. And if you sow goodness, you will reap goodness in the form of inner joy.*
>
> *To understand karma, you must realize that thoughts are things. Matter responds to the power of thought. Will power directs energy, and energy in turn acts upon matter. Matter indeed is energy.*
>
> *Human suffering is not a sign of God's, or Nature's anger with mankind. It is a sign, rather, of man's ignorance of the divine law.*
>
> *We punish ourselves by our own evil actions and reward ourselves by our own good deeds.*
>
> *Sin is a crust which hides the perfect soul, made eternally in the image of God. When that crust is dissolved by meditation, the perfection of the soul is revealed at last.*
>
> *Karma is our own responsibility. Every circumstance in our lives, every characteristic, every habit, however much we now repudiate it was something we ourselves created, whether recently or in the distant past.*
>
> *Only through deep, inner communion with higher states of consciousness does it become clear that all deficiencies, whether mental or physical, are the just consequences of a person's misbehavior in the past. A wise sage has the inner clarity to perceive the exact cause of every mishap. He can then prescribe actions that will remove that cause as an influence in a person's life.*
>
> *There are no obstacles; There are only opportunities.*
>
> *The more we live guided from within, the greater our control over outer events in the great game of life.*

Once the ego has been transcended in soul-consciousness, however, the realm of karmic law is transcended also. The soul remains forever unaffected, for karmic consequences accrue only to the ego.

In Self-realization, the soul is released at last from its bondage to karmic law.

Immortality of the Soul

If an immortal soul has not worked out in one lifetime of school those delusions which bind him, he needs more lifetimes of schooling to bring him the understanding of his innate immortality.

Ordinary souls, therefore reincarnate, compelled by their earth-bound desires. Great souls, on the other hand, come on earth only partly to work out their karma, but principally to act as noble sons of God to show lost children the way to their heavenly Father's home.

When God sees that a soul, by the misuse of free will and bad company, has lost itself in the forest of egotism, He becomes very concerned for him, and sends him spiritual aid to bring him back into His fold of divine, virtuous living. He helps souls to reincarnate in places where they can work out their karma and liberate their souls by meditation and wisdom.

Reincarnation and the Hindu Teachings

The Hindu scripture, the Bhagavad Gita describes reincarnation as a wheel constantly turning.

Reincarnation teaches that life continues after so-called death. The body does not last but the soul lasts forever – the permanent soul in a temporary body. The soul cannot go back to God until it reaches perfection. Hence, when the body perishes, the soul must have another body in order to overcome its imperfections.

Souls who fail to preserve their perfection while in the mortal school of education and entertainment have to come back for many incarnations until they experience completely their hidden Spirit nature. The immortal soul must win several prizes in order to maintain Spirit-endurance: ***self-control, detachment, morality, calmness, and spirituality*** *– and must pass all grades in the earthly school in order to become free.*

Unless its material desires are cast off before death, the soul must return to another body in the earthly moving picture house in order to work out the desires born there.

If the perfect soul-children of God come on earth and do everything to please God rather than to satisfy the craving of their ego, then they will be free from the necessity for reincarnation.

Edgar Cayce and Reincarnation

Edgar Cayce - (March 18, 1877 – January 3, 1945) was an American clairvoyant who answered questions on subjects as varied as healing, **reincarnation**, wars, Atlantis, and future events while claiming to be in a trance. A biographer gave him the nickname, "The Sleeping Prophet". Throughout his life, Cayce was drawn to church as a member of the Disciples of Christ. He read the Bible once a year every year, taught at Sunday school, and recruited missionaries. He said he could see auras around people, spoke to angels, and heard voices of departed relatives.

At first his readings of **reincarnations** went against his biblical teachings and at one point he wanted to cease his channeling sessions. Cayce lost his voice and in a reading for himself, he was informed if he was no longer going to be a channel, his mission in this life was complete. Ultimately his trance voice, the "we" of the readings, dialogued with Cayce and finally persuaded him to continue with reincarnation readings.

The Great Depression years saw Cayce turn his attention to spiritual teachings. In 1931, Edgar Cayce's friends and family asked him how they could become psychic like him. Out of this seemingly simple question came an eleven-year discourse that led to the creation of "Study Groups". From his altered state, Cayce relayed to this group that the purpose of life is not to become psychic, but to become a more spiritually aware and loving person. Study Group #1 was told that they could "bring light to a waiting world" and that these lessons would still be studied a hundred years into the future. The readings were now about dreams, coincidence (synchronicity), developing intuition, karma, the **akashic records**, astrology, **past-life relationships, soul mates** and other esoteric subjects. Hundreds of books have been published about these readings.

We know from the study of Cayce's readings and other sources that successive future incarnations should have at least five key points of similarity:

1. Astrology
2. Facial Appearance
3. Karmic traits and lessons
4. Karmic places
5. Karmic people

Astrology is vitally important in terms of the spiritual "configuration" of an entity. Therefore, we should see remarkable astrological similarities between successive incarnations.

The facial appearance is another vital "stamp" of an entity's own identity that transcends the space of one simple lifetime. The entity's innate personal vibrations determine the precise arrangement of the DNA molecule. Therefore, we should expect that successive incarnations have obvious facial similarities.

We frequently reincarnate to redo karmic patterns:

The entity will invariably have the same traits, both "good" and "bad," and therefore be drawn back into learning the same karmic lessons, repeating them again and again until they are mastered.

Henri René Albert Guy de Maupassant (5 August 1850 – 6 July 1893) was a popular 19th-century French writer and considered one of the fathers of the modern short story. He was highly promiscuous and died early of syphilis.

He reincarnated as Penny's mother, (3 August 1913-1996) who was an avid reader including the works of de Maupassant. (Widowed in her 30's she never dated again.)

The entity might well be drawn back into the same places that it had lived in the past.

The entity will invariably be drawn back into associations with the same people that it had known in the past, reincarnating with them again in the future.

- Many souls incarnate in order to make better choices in life that lead to higher understanding and vibration of consciousness.
- Others choose to take a different route in order to balance karma or gain different experiences and learn compassion.
- Some choose to finish lessons not completed in one lifetime to be carried on in another.
- Since many of us decide to incarnate together for the purpose of growth and transformation, when you find others that you have been with before, there is a high probability that this is not the first experience together.
- Frequently it is through the eyes of others that we are able to discern the colors and textures of life that go unrecognized alone. By blending and merging with others that have agreed to share experiences on the earth plane, we are able to recognize and embrace more than if this were a solitary journey. It is a group process and a higher form of teaching and learning.

David Wilcock

Renown psychic, David Wilcock confronted his readings about the reincarnation issue on November 27, 1997, and they confirmed that it was true, and "with this knowledge comes responsibility — great responsibility." The readings told him that he was "not as configured this time for medical readings" and should devote his time to "teaching universal concepts to the masses." David had a hard time believing what they told him and was slightly argumentative as the reading came in. Soon after this, David began having specific dreams that detailed various aspects of Cayce's life, and he gradually accepted his reincarnation as fact.

David decided to cast a comparison chart between the time of Edgar Cayce's birth and that of his own. He was shocked to see the similarity between the two charts. All of the inner planets were in almost the exact same positions on the two charts, and the outer planets were in near-perfect aspects to each other such as square, trine and sextile.

He later realized that both he and Cayce were born in the Year of the Ox in the Chinese Zodiac, and that the vertices or "balance points" of the two charts were in a perfect 180-degree opposition.

in January 2000, world-famous psychic Uri Geller also confirmed that David was Edgar Cayce's reincarnation and Geller publicized it on his website.

David Wilcock is a professional lecturer, filmmaker and researcher of ancient civilizations, consciousness science and new paradigms of energy and matter. He is rewriting entire branches of science and leading a new narrative of human history, one that includes races of highly advanced beings that we share earth and space with. The Golden thread that weaves his work together is the science of Ascension - a solar-system-wide transformation that elevates earth and humanity to a higher phase of spiritual advancement. David's message is one of unity and love, encouraging people to live a life of goodness and harmony. He is a cosmic reporter of poignant news and events in the Ascension timeline and drama.

www.divinecosmos.com

Soul Groups/Soul Mates

- Our soul group/mates come to earth with us and some of them work behind the scenes on other dimensions. They come as mothers, fathers, teachers, friends, the plumber etc. that are here to grow, learn, and ascend together.
- Any soul that you connect with deeply could be considered a "soul mate." People can have many soul mates. Usually, they are individuals who have similar rays and spiritual paths, and often have been together for many lifetimes off and on.
- Since many of us decide to incarnate together for the purpose of growth and transformation, when you find others that you have been with before, there is a high probability that this is not the first experience together.
- The path from lifetime to lifetime is not necessarily a straight line and can include many branches; all working on different aspects of soul growth. Therefore, there may be several souls incarnate at a time that can trace their "ancestry" back to a historical figure in a previous lifetime.
- Claire Heartsong has pointed out in her book *Anna – the Voice of the Magdalenes* that perhaps the reason why so many of us believe we were Mary Magdalene or are drawn to this work and teachings is that we were part of the Magdalene Order which also included men.
- These seeds of Light were planted in the cellular memory and are finally sprouting and shining forth in the flowering of awareness that this is the time for fulfillment of the Christ-Magdalene blueprint: the divine masculine and the divine feminine blueprint of Divine Union, which realizes finally the truth of the wholeness within: The Sacred Marriage within.
- It is believed by many scholars that it was the eruption of violence as perpetrated by the newer, male-dominated cultures that obliterated the peaceful, earth-honoring ways of Goddess worship and honoring of the Divine Mother and paved the way for the strong hold of Christianity and eventually the obliteration of the Goddess from religion, religious texts and teachings.

In this millennium we are seeing a resurgence of the Divine Feminine and an observance of the feminine as sacred. We are seeing her in history, art, folklore, religion, spirituality, archeology, media, and mythology. Today many refer to the Divine as Mother-Father God.

My guides have described it as similar to a kaleidoscope – souls are together in a pattern then the times shift, and they are reformed into different patterns with the same souls.

Soul Rays

- Different souls radiate different attributes and archetypes of Creation. There is a color scheme that describes the major archetypes. It is the same one used in the chakra system. "Red" tends to mean very passionate and physical, "orange" very social, "yellow" intellectual, "green" Earthy and healing-oriented, "blue" conceptual and mental, "indigo" intuitive and psychic and "violet" higher wisdom and transcendence.
- Your lifetime theme or ray is a choice to experience the energy of that particular ray in form. We are a weaving of Rays: we have the personality ray(s), soul ray, and monadic ray - so with different "levels" of consciousness and spiritual evolution as we unfold utilizes different rays more prominently.
- Different incarnations of a soul may be experienced in different rays, even simultaneously.

Split Aparts/Twin Flames

- Greek philosopher, Plato (427 BC-348 BC). Plato's theory was that each human being is part of one soul, but they are only half of that one. The idea is that the soul was "split-apart" and separated from each other– and, since that time, the two halves have been forever searching for one another in order to join together and regain their sense of original created wholeness.
- Each of these alleged halves of the one soul learns all of life's lessons at their own pace, and if the two halves happen to cross paths at some point during life, they may have a powerful bond; because they are each other's "split-apart".
- They may find a truly genuine connection, they're so alike in emotions or issues, that in some cases it's too much for them to handle.
- Just because someone is a split-apart does not mean that you will get along with them. Everyone has their good side and a bad side, so it is only reasonable to believe if one "part of the soul" inherits the most of either that the other will have the majority of the other.

I find it interesting that Paul and I incarnated at the exact same moment in time "Across the Universe" from each other with different abilities to experience life in different forms.

Though we may bring many similarities as mentioned above, we have chosen to experience them in different expressions in the world of form.

Perhaps it is good we have never met...

Soul Braids or Walk-Alongs

"Souls are individuations of the Divine Cosmic Intelligence and are therefore multidimensional. It may be hard for some to fathom that humans have counterparts that exist in other planes and realms of consciousness where there is peaceful cooperation among all beings of light. In this century, we are seeing a lot of changes on Earth, as well as in our experience as humans. One of those changes is the incoming of multidimensional aspects of our souls. These are called "soul braids" or "walk-alongs" in which the energy of an additional soul joins the Earth mission, but the original personality/soul does not leave. Instead, the two souls integrate. There may be name changes as a result. There are certainly physical, emotional, and cognitive changes. Sometimes companion souls move in and out of the body as needed. One will hold the body while the other takes care of matters in another dimension or level of vibrational consciousness, and then swap places or peacefully cohabitate and collaborate on a project for which both souls are needed.

Soul braids can be formed in any number of combinations. Sometimes a soul braid is an Oversoul merge in which a higher aspect of the same soul will download into the body and become part of a life experience, either temporarily or lifelong. An Oversoul is a future self or higher frequency (think of musical or vibrational octaves) that is purer in consciousness and free of the polarity that characterizes three-dimensional life on Earth. When someone is said to be living in the third dimension, it means they are operating from the lower three chakras and have no concept of their multi-dimensional aspects.

There are cases when two or more souls may share a body, or its electromagnetic field, for a season or a lifetime. Entities, which are both detrimental and beneficial soul aspects, can attach themselves to the body or aura of an incarnated soul. When two or more enlightened or evolved souls share a body or auric space, there is the kind of cooperation, peace, and harmony that we humans experience when working on a project as a team. By the same token, there are cases in which we see lower aspects of a soul attached to and influencing an embodied soul. We want to avoid this and free ourselves of the potential for this to occur. When we forgive others, we heal wounds and close the portals that allow such contamination.

Like the Christ, we raise our vibration by focusing on joy and bliss and by recognizing our oneness with God and All That Is—even these lower aspects of our souls. When we "cast them out" we are actually integrating them or putting them into their proper perspective by not allowing them to rule and reign over our thoughts, emotions, and actions. Then, the higher avatar self takes the wheel and calls the shots."

Yvonne Perry, *Shifting into Soul Consciousness*,

http://integratingfrequencies.blogspot.com/2014/12/soul-braids-or-walk-alongs.html

Soul Groups

"Together, you all have a specific mission and purpose to achieve that is part of a greater and bigger vision for the Universe.

All the members of your Soul Group vibrate within a certain frequency and your soul is in harmony with that vibration. Your Soul Group is often chosen by you before you were born as it is believed to support your soul and its mission and growth in this lifetime.

You may not meet all the members of your Soul Group in this lifetime, but regardless you are all working towards the same goal or mission here on Earth while bringing your own unique flavor and personality to the process.

Members of your Soul Group come into your life to change your world and to expand your mind. They also come to remind you of your journey, purpose and mission.

Some people identify members of their Soul Group as Soulmates, as often there is a strong chemistry, connection or familiarity upon meeting.

There are different levels or types of Soulmates that we can encounter which could be presented to us as family members, romantic partners, teachers, enemies and even chance encounters."

source; foreverconscious.com

Karma

Karma is a word from the philosophy of many Indian religions (Hinduism, Buddhism, Jainism, Sikhism). The basic theory is that the universe runs according to certain laws, all described by one word 'Dharma' (Sanskrit) or 'Dhamma' (Pali). The basic theory is: cause and effect'. The laws (Dharma) decide what effect is beget from a given cause. Karma is the cause part of this theory. In other words, your actions - mental, vocal and physical are your Karma (plural). In the Buddhist philosophy, Dharma does not 'punish' or 'reward' anyone. The concepts of good and bad don't exist here.

According to Edgar Cayce, a 20th century American mystic, Karma is the meeting of oneself in the present through thoughts and deeds from the past. Karma is tied to the concept of reincarnation and balance. Karma's purpose is not simply to cause suffering, but to give the individual an opportunity to experience every aspect of life. For instance, if a person has wronged someone in a past life, he will be given the opportunity to experience being wronged, and can also experience the resolving of issues, traits, and tendencies as well.

Talents and skills are never lost when a person completes an incarnation, according to the Cayce files. Someone who has developed an ability in one life will still have it to draw upon later through karma. One may be born, for example, as a genius or prodigy, in math for example, if he develops this skill or has been of service now or having done so to a prodigious degree in the past or present.

Reactions to past thoughts and actions become our fate, destiny and karma. An individual's fate is simply the rebounding effects of previous choices remembered by its soul. The reason the effects of these previous choices often seem unfair to the conscious mind is because the personality doesn't see beyond its own life for sources of current conditions.

Karma has been described as memory. Karma is memory coming to consciousness again. What has occurred in the past is recalled and has an effect on the present. It is a pool of information that the subconscious mind draws upon and can utilize in the present. It has elements that are positive as well as those which may seem negative.

One of the most distorted views of karma is the idea that nothing can be done about it, similar to the concept of destiny. No matter how terrible the predicament, there is always something that can be done to resolve the situation, even if it's a patient smile and maintaining a positive attitude in the face of adversity.

The law also works in some very curious ways. Somehow one's greatest weakness possesses the potential to become one's greatest strength. With each difficult situation, whether physical, mental or spiritual, there comes an opportunity. These "opportunities" sometimes appear to be hopeless problems, like a crippling disease, an uncontrollable habit or a situation in which one feels totally victimized without cause. More often they appear as annoyances or frustrations, like an unattractive nose, a difficult sibling, spouse, colleague, boss, lover or friend; or an ever-present lack of money. In each case, the soul has an opportunity to resolve and overcome some weakness in itself, and by doing so with the right attitude, the soul can rise to new heights of consciousness, love, and companionship.

Spiritual teacher, **Michael Mirdad**, shared in a talk on Karma versus Grace at Unity of Sedona: He began by explaining that karma is simply the law of cause and effect; whatever we put out-in thought, word, or deed tends to come back to us in one form or another. And reincarnation is simply the continuation of karma from one lifetime to another. Then he explained that, although people tend to think that when we experience the effect of something we "caused," the karma is complete. But this is actually not the case. The cycle continues until there is forgiveness. Then Michael explained that forgiveness is not the same as grace. Instead, forgiveness is an expression of Grace. Grace is how God Loves us. Forgiveness is how we love each other. And as we practice forgiveness, it opens us up to the Light of Grace that shines upon us and awakens us to our true identity. When we are in a state of Grace, we are in a state of Love--back to our Real Self.

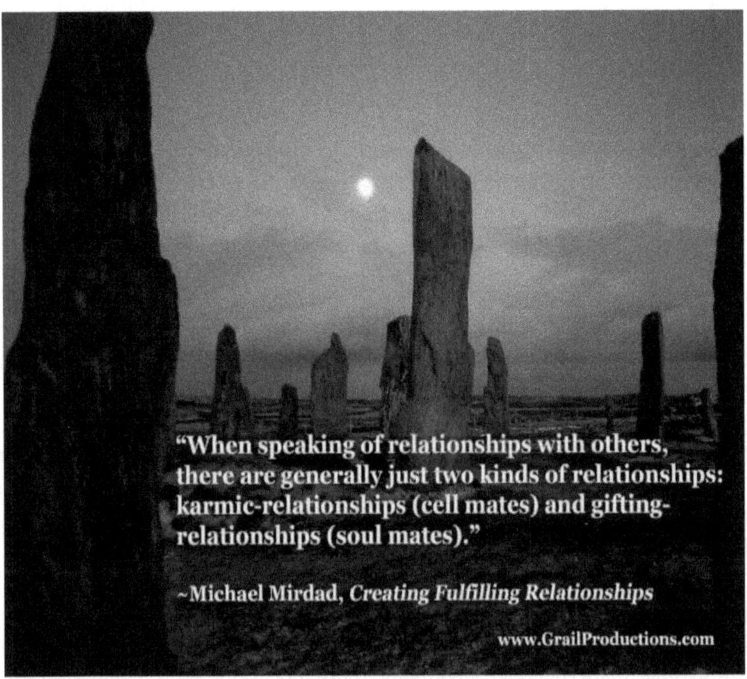

Coming together of Science, Psychology, and Spirituality

Brian L Weiss, M.D.

Dr. Weiss pioneered regression therapy – guiding people through their past lives. As a traditional psychotherapist, Dr. Weiss was astonished and skeptical when one of his patients began recalling past-life traumas that seemed to hold the key to her recurring nightmares and anxiety attacks. His skepticism was eroded, however when she began to channel messages from the "space between lives" which contained remarkable revelations about Dr. Weiss' family and his dead son. Using past-life therapy, he was able to cure the patient and embark on a new, more meaningful phase in his own career. His many books, CD's and workshops guide others on this unique path of discovery.

www.brianweiss.com

Michael Newton, M.D.

When Dr. Michael Newton, a certified Master Hypnotherapist, began regressing his clients back in time to access their memories of former lives, he stumbled onto a discovery of enormous proportions: that it is possible to see into the spirit world through the mind's eye of subjects who are in a hypnotized or superconscious state; and that clients in this altered state were able to tell him what their soul was doing between lives on Earth. His book, *Journey of Souls*, 1994, *presents* ten years of his research and insights to help people understand the purpose behind their life choices, and how and why our soul - and the souls of those we love - lives eternally.

www.spiritualregression.org,

My Journey

I believed in reincarnation in an abstract way but saw little relevance to my life today. That was then, and this is now. I lived in the moment so what difference did it make?

That was until 2006... I was awakened in the night and led to a book on my shelf about Renoir, the impressionist painter. Turning to the *Luncheon of the Boating Party*, I knew who I was in the painting and was soon to know who all of the other people were as well, and who they had reincarnated into in my life now.

That expanded as I explored the well-documented era and portraits of others in that significant time in history. I began to realize that I was part of a soul group that incarnated then and had come back together in Albuquerque/Santa Fe, New Mexico and Sedona. I discuss this in more depth in the chapter about Paul Lhote.

If we were together then, there was a high probability that we had been together in other lifetimes as well. I knew I had been part of the Essenes at the time of Jesus and so I began asking who else I knew was there as well. I began compiling a complex "family tree" of those I knew who had been part of that soul group. Over 250 names and faces were on the original chart and I continue to add others as they appear in my life. I talk more about this lifetime in the chapter on Jesus and my life as Mary Jacobe Cleopas.

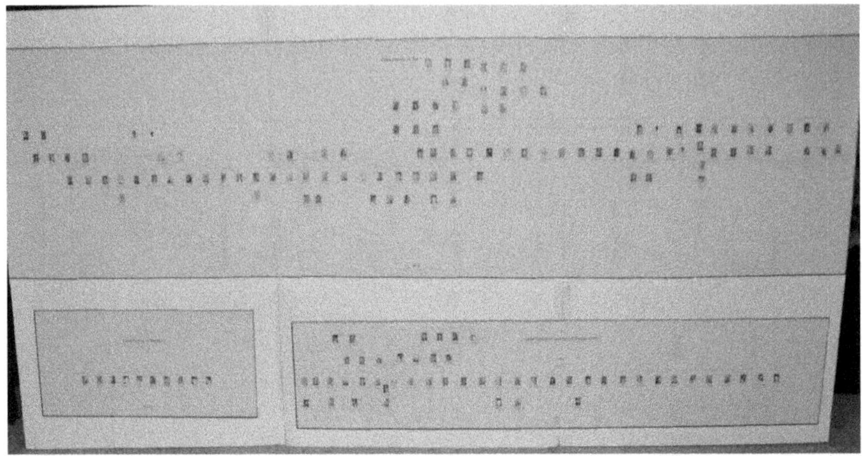

Edgar Cayce talked about how we are drawn to locales where we have experienced different lifetimes. I began to think of the times I have been unknowingly drawn back to England and France many times and the many lifetimes I experienced there. I live in the southwest and have experienced other lifetimes here as a Native American. My interest in and visit to China retraced Chinese lifetimes. My travels in New England and life in Washington DC and Virginia must have drawn me back to lifetimes experienced there in the 1700's. I have been reluctant to go to Germany, which probably has something to do with my death at Dachau. It is as if we are energetically wired to the frequency of the places in our soul history.

My themes in this lifetime and threads I bring from those before are around beauty, artistic expression, and communication – clairaudience, writing, speaking, teaching, designing and bringing people together. There is a spiritual thread that runs through all of my incarnations that seems to reflect and make sense of the world in transition. I see and hear things others may not and must find ways to communicate it to those around me in order to help us all evolve. I am here to help make the world a more beautiful place and to help others see the face of God reflected in the beauty around us.

I am a clear channel, proficient dowser, and calibrate truth on the numeric energetic scale described by Dr. David Hawkins in his book Power vs Force. I get "downloads" of knowing and verify the impressions I am getting with kinesiology and calibration of the energetic vibration of the information. I am able to ask questions and get clear answers from across the veil, especially about events that are in my akashic records. I have written several books with my partners in spirit and now it seems they have more information for me to bring forth...

People tell me they do not "remember" their previous lives and neither do I. I do not "relive" previous incarnations in my mind or see a "movie" of significant scenes. I "get" downloads of awareness in tiny pieces that I begin to research using kinesiology. I will "know" that something is significant because I know it to be so, even though I may have no frame of reference in this lifetime. I begin to ask questions of my higher self with kinesiology and access my akashic records in that way. By continuing to ask questions, clearer pictures emerge.

If we are not new souls, and I do not believe I am, we have had thousands of lifetimes to bring us to our present state of being. At first, I was concerned that these were mostly famous people that I was identifying with. Most believe that that is highly improbable given the number of possibilities involved. I asked if I was just picking up on the archetype of these people and was told that I was not. I do believe that I carry the Akashic records of these lifetimes in my DNA, **as do many others.** Since I embody aspects of that past-life experience, I am able to tap into and apply lessons learned and integrate this into my life today. These incarnations were chosen because they all were harbingers of times of change and illumination. They said that I was "a fly on the wall" at these times of great change so that I could tell the tale. If that is so, that is what I am doing...

I do not claim to be the ONLY incarnation of these entities. As others have explained, we carry our akashic records of all our past-life experiences in our DNA as part of our cellular memory. We share pieces of DNA with thousands of others who may have descended from the same source. There may be others in this lifetime who share DNA of that same entity but are choosing to live out different color soul rays in this one or are simply unaware of the source of their current experiences.

I ask only that you keep an open mind and see how this explains many "coincidences" and passions in your life.

Patterns

One of the "patterns" I see emerging is the progression of themes of lifetimes. Souls coming in begin at the bottom and learn how to navigate the world, satisfying survival issues and clashes with egos and ideals. As we refine these, we move into the realm of relationships and spiritual understanding. It seems to follow the patterns Maslow identified in his hierarchy of needs diagram.

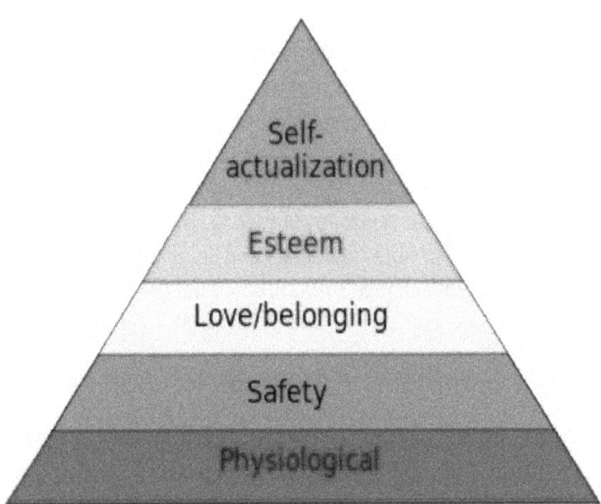

I have surveyed other members of my soul group who have made their missteps, learned the lessons, moved up the pyramid, and are operating from a higher level of awareness. I am grateful to be able to share their insights as well as my own.

Soul Weaving

We are a tapestry of our experiences interwoven with others who have shared our path. I am fortunate to have many friends in my soul group who I have shared previous lives with and they are aware of the process. I asked them to share their awareness of any of them that I have identified as significant for me that they were also part of.

When I say I "get" something, it is a "knowing" that appears in my consciousness that I confirm with kinesiology and I test the energetic vibration. The image I get of it is of the chunk of my cellular memory lying dormant in the bottom of my awareness. Occasionally pieces break off and bubble to the surface as "knowing". As in the fable of the blind men and the elephant, if we each describe what we "see" and experience, a clearer picture will emerge.

I asked others I know as part of my soul group if they have any recollection or knowing about any of the lives we might have experienced together. Here are their responses...

The Cast of Characters

Teresa - The first to respond was Teresa. She is a quiet soul with tremendous depth. She is not originally from the US but has lived here many years. She has been a Rosicrucian in this lifetime and is blessed to be able to read Akashic records of our soul's journey that is found in our DNA. I was amazed at the number of lifetimes we have shared and delighted with the details she was able to access from them.

> *" To my understanding, groups of souls are put together by family ties, friendships, and to support each other in missions for one purpose that serves the Highest Will. At this time Earth is passing through a stage that will define a future into a Higher Dimensions and where, or how, our true essence is.*
> *Namaste....Om...."*

Janice is a conscious friend I got to know in Albuquerque. We realized we had spent many lifetimes together and were able to access some of them.

> *"I do think that it is almost beyond comprehension at the way our souls have interconnected in various lifetimes. I can remember lifetimes beyond Earth, as well, most importantly my lifetimes on the Pleiades which is known for its great artisans, singers, dancers, and joyful Souls.*
>
> *We who are sensitive and aware of our lifetimes do gather and immediately "recognize" each other. While we may meet now, passing through each other's*

lives, even briefly, there is always that deep soul remembrance...as Proust put it: "The Remembrance of Things Past".

I know I am "on" the Red Ray, working with the Blue Ray, and that El Morya is my Higher Self. No shock there, as he was a "task master" ...a strong force indeed... something I have had to temper in this life! I wanted to deny it in many ways after I became so anti-war/military, but I have made "peace" with it. (I was also General Patton...another "gung-ho, gung- ho" military man. Another lifetime I want to put behind me (although I realize we experience different lives to get the full feeling of "being human" in all its forms). Life is amazingly complex, beautiful, and yet, at times very exasperating!"

Gordon was my soulmate and husband that transitioned from this world in 2005. We have shared many lifetimes. I believe he had previous incarnations as and carried the DNA of the Apostle Matthew (Levi), Charlemagne, St. Francis of Assisi, and George Washington among others.

Will helped me navigate the waters following Gordon's transition and get my "sea legs" in a world without him, including putting a business to rest. We have spent several lifetimes together, many with him as my guide and protector.

Will grew up near Roswell New Mexico and has had experiences with UFO's and abductions. He has facilitated groups of paranormal explorers that attempt to put together pieces of hidden knowledge others have tried to obscure. He currently facilitates a metaphysical exploration group in northern New Mexico.

Will does not consciously have any recollection of specifics around the lifetimes we have shared but agrees with me that we were there together at several times in history including at the time of Jesus, as Knights Templar, with Joan of Arc, and in the Impressionist period.

Bo showed up in this lifetime after my husband died. We have spent many lifetimes together – usually with him as my champion and protector for he carries that energy. In this lifetime he was a marine and Pentecostal minister who can quote most passages from the Bible and does so frequently. He is probably one of the most well-read and self-taught men I have ever known. In his learning, he became a "born-again Gnostic" and was asked to leave the fundamentalist church when he continued to ask the hard questions. We have shared many insights and helped each other grow spiritually. He loaded up my belongings and helped me move to Sedona where he has been frequently drawn for renewal.

"One thing that came to me is that we are all connected; we all have a part of each other, a percentage small or large. I think it depends on how much we know the character through the contact of reading, contemplating on them, focusing, channeling, wanting to be them etc."

"I've met many women who claimed they are Mary Magdalene, Mary the mother, Cleopatra, etc. One that comes to mind swears she's Magdalene 100% in the flesh. I told her to be careful about losing her own identity of who she was. She never talked to me again! Seems like this has been an occurrence throughout my journey, go figure, huh? "

Amara has been part of many of my lifetimes. When she showed up in this one, we both knew we had to go to France together which we did. She lived in my home in New Mexico and we shared many adventures.

Don I shared a home with Don for five years in Sedona. I believe we have shared many lifetimes including ones with Jesus, as a Knight's Templar, Joan of Arc, and with Victor Hugo. I see the patterns of heroism, honor and knighthood, and writing that weave together in his life experiences. His book ***A Matter of Time*** shares his adventures in the criminal "justice" system. While he says he believes in reincarnation, he does not spend a lot of time exploring these patterns because he is too busy creating new ones.

Jami is a beautiful sister of Light that I have had a privilege of sharing a house with for 1-1/2 years. A former Science of Mind minister, hospice worker, healer, musician and "fairy" on so many levels. She lights up my life and that of many others in our soul group.

"Since meeting Penny and attending community gatherings and events she has hosted or helped to present, and by living with her as a housemate, many pieces have come together for me, of my past, or other aspects of myself within other time lines of my soul's experience. I have had opportunity to remember more of my soul's lineage and to meet the people that were also a part of those times. I have been able to do my work to love, forgive, accept and evolve what may have been incomplete or out of balance within my experiences with people from this group of souls. I experience all of us committed to do our work to understand, allow, love and forgive each other, including ourselves, for the imbalances or aches from the past lives and other timeline experiences.

Up to this point of meeting Penny, I certainly had been connecting with familiar souls in my life, and plenty of opportunity to bring old things into new light, but things quantum leaped when moving to Sedona and quickly meeting many people from my Soul Group of powerful evolutionary and transforming lifetimes. Many of us seemed to move to Sedona about the same time as well, reminding me that nothing is ever coincidence and a divine plan indeed calls us together again to do the work we incarnate together to do.

Dave Dr. Michael Newman talks about when we are in the bardo (intermediate state between lifetimes) we agree on a sign, so we can recognize each other after we incarnate. I believe I have shared 10 lifetimes with Dave. In this one, when we met he said he saw lights in my eyes, like he had never seen before. We recognized each other immediately. We are very different. Mother Mary Anna has said we are like yin/yang, mirror images and help fill in missing pieces in each other's puzzle. Frequently we have been on opposing sides of an issue in order to mirror greater understanding. He is a "brother" and we share a household along with other conscious "siblings".

Dave's background includes a master's degree in Biblical studies and a time spent as a Pentecostal preacher. He served 20 years in the National Guard. He was a conservative, Republican State Senator for twelve years but has shifted from those early years and now embraces a new-age philosophy that takes him deep into many rabbit holes in spiritually-active Sedona and beyond the stars. He is an advanced student in the Course in Miracles and leads workshops around the country that marry the origins and understanding of the world money systems, releasing ourselves from financial slavery, and reordering our relationship to financial wealth to transform humanity.

> *"During most of my life I had accepted what I was taught the reincarnation was just a Hindu/Eastern belief and was not accepted by Christians. Being a seminary graduate, I accepted that belief for over 30 years. After a dramatic change in my life I began to question many of my past beliefs, wanting to have a better understanding of life. I was in session with others as we were with a wonderful woman who channeled the archangels. It was there I went through a change and began to understand from a broader perspective about past lives.*
>
> *So I delved in and purchased as audiotape of a self-meditative session on past lives. It was about 1 1/2 hours long and at the end it asked us to feel, sense and trust what was coming forward.*
>
> *The impressions came that I was an arms dealers/manufacturer in Germany in the late 1800's. I was extremely wealthy, loved by the king, but in my later life suffered from serve depression and guilt for what I had done. I had become a manufacturer of murder and war bringing about great suffering and bloodshed.*
>
> *I kept this to myself, until about 5 years later I was discussing this with a friend, she pointed at me with and with wide alert eyes she said, "you were Alfred Krupp and you just described who he was." This spurned an interest, as I then delved into his life, purchased four books on the Krupp family and learned how he was the one who birthed the early beliefs of the rise of Nazism and the holocaust.*
>
> *Later, I had a personal session with the woman who did the angel channelings. During that time, I enquired why I had this deep love for Jesus/Jeshua since I was a small boy. The angel came through and said it was because I was there with him. I was present at the crucifixion and the resurrection. My name was Merilius, the Lieutenant Centurion of Palestine. I was the head soldier in the*

region. I had quietly become friends with him and he had a huge impact on my life after his resurrection. This has been confirmed many times by others in the past years.

The intertwining and coincidence in these two lifetimes is understood in living karmic cycles. The Romans were hated with a deep passion by the Jews during the times of Jeshua. Collectively they had a very deep hatred toward me as the head Roman soldier. As Alfred Krupp, that karmic cycle came full circle as being one who helped birth the holocaust."

Jewels is a professor in the Masters in Transpersonal Psychology program at Atlantic University, which was founded by Edgar Cayce. Previously, she was a professor of education and a teacher of young children for 21 years. Jewels has lived in Sedona, Arizona since 2001 when she became an Usui Reiki Master and began working as a healer and guide to the tremendous vortex energies in the sacred site of Sedona. She is a conscious channel for The Christ-Magdalene energies of healing, inspiration, and love. Her book, ***Mary Magdalene: The Christos-Sophia Revelation*** calibrates at 1,000 on David Hawkins scale. She is also the author of ***Every Child is Holy, Soul Songs***, and co-author of ***The Crystal Skull Messenger***. We have shared many lifetimes

Nancy was a shamanic practitioner and professional guide on the land of the beautiful red rocks and vortices, before she began working with the feminine and the Magdalene Mysteries. She has been facilitating women's circles and guiding men and women on pilgrimages to sacred sites in southern France, as a bilingual guide and has been a researcher of the legacies and mysteries Mary Magdalene, the Knights Templar and the Cathars left there long ago. She is a French Knight's Templar. Her latest book is ***A Magdalene Awakens: Hidden Temple Secrets.***

Vicky was born in Egypt in this lifetime but knows that she has had many more there and in Italy.

Jeff has shared many lives with me and we cross paths again in Sedona.

Susan is a spiritual teacher and a "walk-in".

Kevin and I have shared several lifetimes, including ones at the time of Jesus where he was Judas Iscariot. This gave him a lot of concern when he first discovered this. He relates that experience in his book, ***Trust, Patience, Surrender***. We have been able to discuss it and put it into perspective and make sense of the implications and lessons. All is not as it seems on the surface. I know we have also shared previous lifetimes in France where he has traveled and volunteered at Lourdes in this one.

Michael is a spiritual teacher and author of many spiritual books.

Victoria and I have shared 10 lifetimes. She continues to grow and express her magnificent abilities and understandings in Sedona.

Jeri and I have shared many lifetimes. A former psychologist, she has written many "fiction" books including ***Return of the Goddess – the Hidden History of Nefertiti, Akhenaten, Mary Magdalene and Scotia*** that allow her to tell stories that bring light to history.

Margaret is a soul sister who has studied many spiritual paths in our walk together.

Harry Before I met Harry in this lifetime Mother Mary Anna told me that a beloved was coming who would be "rekindling fires left burning in previous lifetimes". She was right, and I have shared many of our experiences in my book ***Hieros Gamos – the Sacred Union of the Divine Feminine and Divine Masculine***. He has no conscious recollection of any of them but is quite sensitive to locations and emotions surrounding past associations. We continue to stoke the fires of loving awareness, which indeed heals all wounds

Joy – is a soul sister I have only recently reconnected with though we have spent many lifetimes together. We are both Chaplains at Unity and again work together healing, teaching, and counseling others on the spiritual path.

Barbara is an accomplished and clear channel of the spiritual realms. She works with many to remove blocks that prevent them accessing their higher powers. She provides voice and guidance from Mary Magdalene to those in our sisterhood.

Harmony - is an accomplished healer and massage therapist. She was the first one I connected with in Sedona and has been a valued friend ever since.

Kathleen is an author and researcher. Though our paths have never crossed physically in this lifetime – only on-line, I believe we have shared many lifetimes and experiences.

Derek is a soul brother I have yet to meet, as our paths have not crossed physically in this lifetime. I know we were best friends in the Impressionist lifetime and share similar interests born in that epoch. He has reached out to me in his books for over 30 years which I am led to read, and he writes about places that we are both drawn to, for which I am very grateful.

Azura is a gifted spiritual teacher and channel who shared our house in Sedona.

Joel is an author and teacher of sacred concepts.

Elizabeth was an extraordinary poet, professor and Shakespearean scholar that I had the fortune of sharing several lives with, including this one in Sedona.

John When I met John and his wife Elizabeth several years ago when they moved to Sedona there was an instant recognition in all of us that we had shared many past lives together. John is a beautiful soul and an extraordinary artist who continues to enrich all of our lives.

Lanna is a prolific seeker of spiritual wisdom, objects and students on the path. She is another Gemini who helps weave together people and understanding.

Loras is a sculptor of copper representations of sacred geometry.

Shelly is new to the sisterhood in this lifetime but we have trod this path together before.

Jayana is a professor and teacher of world religions. She is the author of the "fiction" book, ***The Ultimate Love Story*** about Jesus and Mary Magdalene in India and France.

Jim I never met him in this lifetime though I "get" we have shared 10 lives at other times. He has been a significant figure in previous lives and I was told he would be showing up again in this one to continue our journey together. I expected him to arrive in 2012. I kept looking... In 2014 he committed suicide, unable to step into the role we planned before incarnation. Lots more to do on the other side before we will be together again...

"An invisible red thread
connects those who are
destined to meet, regardless of
time, place, or circumstance.
The thread may stretch or
tangle, but will never break."
–An ancient Chinese belief

Sifting the Sand of Truth

> *"Having power does not make you an expert on truth, nor does it even give you the real truth, for truth comes from God. It does allow you, however to manipulate truth and to enforce whatever truth you believe on others."*
>
> Sylvia Browne, *The Two Marys.*

> *"All history is a myth, a story created to make some sense out of the few events we know. The past is a hypothesis erected to explain and justify the present."*
>
> Michael Baigent, *The Jesus Papers*

Given the number of theories, options and possibilities of events, how do you discern the Truth? Belief is different from Truth. Almost any hypothesis can be "proven" by "facts" in evidence and therefore believed. However, a personal belief that something is a fact does not make it True. Truth can only be proven on an energetic scale. If belief is relative to the awareness of the experiencer, is there a common consensus of Truth based on commonly held beliefs?

One of the more significant tools I have been able to utilize in coming to terms with the options I am faced with is the use of **Kinesiology** or energy dowsing. I first began using these tools in working with flower remedies, which react with the energy pathways in the body. Kinesiology is an effective way of determining the positive or negative effects substances have on the energy body.

An important book that explains the ways we can view Truth is ***Power vs. Force*** by David Hawkins, M.D., PhD. By using tools such as kinesiology or a pendulum, you too can verify the Truths that you hold to be valid in your life. Rather than Truth being black or white it allows you to calibrate the vibration of the situation or answer on a scale from 1 to 1000. This also allows you to break down the components of a statement and determine which parts are True and which fail to measure up.

The power of an oft-repeated lie in propaganda is very effective. Since history is written by the survivors of conflict, and rarely presents a balanced representation, it helps me discern what parts of accepted history are True and what are distortions of the Truth.

In order to discern the Truths in my reality I have become a compulsive tester of the possibilities that I am confronted with. As I read recorded history, much of which is conflicting, I utilize two tools of discernment: (1) a pendulum and (2) a highlighter. I test each alternative and then highlight the one that tests the highest for Truth. In this way I am able to wade through information and determine what I Know to be True. Since I am relatively clear and not attached to outcomes, many in my circle of friends come to me to test the accuracy of something on an energetic scale. It is one way we share our gifts and understanding with each other.

Once you uncover what you believe to be Truth, what do you do with it?

The search for the Grail is part knowledge, but also releasing and forgiving those who we hold responsible for causing us pain in this and past lifetimes. The real treasure that lies hidden is the grace of Loving awareness that we are all One and in helping each other climb the mountain of understanding, we heal and transform both ourselves and the collective in the process.

I believe I have trod these shores before. I Know that I have witnessed and been the recipient of injustices and atrocities in the name of false interpretations of God's word. I know that in many ways this continues today. **It does not matter**. **All that does is how I receive, reflect, and demonstrate Love in my life**. That is the grace of surrender, forgiveness, and coming together in wholeness.

Penny

Some of my previous lifetimes:

Ramtha (35,000 BC) (Lemuria)

The world was introduced to Ramtha in 1986 by JZ Knight with the publication of the "***White Book", Ramtha***. She tells of him appearing in her kitchen and asking her to let him speak through her to bring his message to the world.

He tells of his life after the fall of Lemuria and Atlantis as *"the great Ram of the Hindu people"*.

"I ascended in front of my people on the northeast side of the mount called Indus. My people, who numbered more than two million, were a mixture of Lemurians, the people from Ionia (later to be termed Macedonia (Greece)), and the tribes-people escaping from Atlantia, the land you call Atlantis. It is my people's lineage that now makes up the populace of India, Tibet, Nepal, and southern Mongolia."

According to him *"the Atlantians had begun to understand and use the principles of light. They knew how to transform light into pure energy through what you term lasers. Intellectual science became the religion of Atlantians."*

"The Lemurians were quite different from the Atlantians. Their social system was built upon communication through thought. They had not the advancement of technology, only a great spiritual understanding. They loved an essence that could not be identified. It was a power they called the Unknown God."

When he was a boy, *"life was destitute and very arduous. Atlantia had already lost its technology, for its scientific centers in the north had been destroyed long ago. In their experiments with traveling on light, the Atlantians had pierced the cloud cover that completely surrounded the planet. When they pierced the stratosphere, great waters fell, and freeze occurred, which put most of Lemuria and the northern parts of Atlantis under great oceans. Thus, the people from Lemuria and the north of Atlantia fled to the southern regions of Atlantis."*

He rose out of the gutter to conquer armies, then himself. *"My soul gradually changed the programming in every cellular structure to increase the vibratory rate within them. The more peaceful I became with life, the more that vibration carried through my entire physical arrangement until I became lighter, and lighter, and faster – going from the speed of matter into the speed of light. I had raised my bodily vibration into light and had taken my entire embodiment with me. I became one with the Unknown God."*

"When I was upon your plane, I married not any woman. But on my march many entities gave me their children as a gift of appreciation. For an entity who had never lain with a woman, I had

more children than anyone I knew. And the children were great teachers for me, for in their innocence and purity of spirit, children live a very simple truth."

Reunion

After my husband died in 2005 I had a life reading by a woman who did both astrology and numerology. She said she saw me looking into and getting information from a crystal; not a ball, but more like a brick. I didn't have anything like this at the time but was keeping a commitment to have a booth at the two-week long Gem and Mineral Show in Tucson, AZ and was sure I would find something there.

At the show I began looking around for my stone. There were lots of wonderful crystals there, but none resonated. I remember saying that "if I was to have this, I needed a sign and certainly one I could afford!" The next day "Walter" showed up in my tent. We had a nice conversation and he bought my book. He turned to leave but then turned back. He said he "had just bought this but thought it must be for me." He handed me a spectacular faceted crystal pillar like nothing I had ever seen. I was stunned, thanked him profusely, and he left.

Talking to Will that night, he wanted to know if he was an angel. I said of course not – he didn't have wings and did not look like John Travolta! He wanted to know why I did not invite him to dinner. I said I was too stunned but would if I saw him again.

The next to the last day of the show he did come back into my tent. He said that he had read my book and liked it. I thanked him again and said that I had been so stunned by his generous gift, I had forgotten to invite him to dinner and wondered if he would like to do that. He said that would be nice – he lived a few blocks from the hotel and I could come over and we might *"meditate before we went out."* That was a new line! But I tested energetically and got to go along with it.

I arrived at his modest house in an unassuming neighborhood. He met me at the door and invited me in. The walls of his home were covered with pictures of angels! Specific angels and he knew all of their names. He said that he was "getting" to do an energy practice on me and wanted to know if that would be all right. I checked and got a yes so sat down in a straight-backed chair and he moved around me while I meditated. I had my eyes closed so I did not know exactly what he did but it felt good. After he finished, we went out for a pleasant dinner. When we returned, before we said good night he gave me a small statue of an angel.

While I was at the show I kept smelling something wonderful – coffee? chocolate? – all sorts of wonderful smells I could not place or find out where they were coming from. When I got home, whenever I opened my computer I would smell that smell. Finally, I realized that something was trying to get my attention. I went into a meditative state, connected with my guidance, and asked what was going on.

I learned that Walter was indeed an angel that was sent to upgrade my receptors so that I could receive messages from Ramtha. We had spent two lifetimes together – once 35,000 years ago in Lemuria where he had adopted me along with others, including J Z Knight. The other was in Egypt where he was the hierophant to the Pharaoh. I was his daughter and he had seen to it that I went through the mystery schools there. I spent the next several months receiving channeled messages from him daily that I began compiling into book form. I was told that I was getting these from our Akashic records since his energy was too strong for me to receive directly.

Then I received a "cease and desist" call from J Z Knight's attorney informing me that she was the "unique channel" of Ramtha and had a copyright on the name. I would be prosecuted if I continued to infer that I was channeling that entity!

Whatever!

I briefly toyed with the possibility of changing the name to something like "Hunkra" the Doonesbury spoof, but I decided against it because it seemed more of a childish prank. While I believed this contention to be ludicrous, I had no intention of getting into a court battle with her industry and chose to expend my energies elsewhere.

It was not long before I began receiving messages from Archangels who had no copyright on their names...

Teresa - Recollection of our Lemurian lifetimes...In Lemuria there was not interaction between us.

> *"My job at the time was to work with Crystals. I lived in a grotto where Crystals where huge, People came for one session and stood and handled the crystal they were called to.*
>
> *I met you and worked with you and your crystal that also happened to be part of mine.*
>
> *We were hermaphrodites.*
>
> *I chipped them to a seed then coded them with healing properties that you would need, memory receipts, and programs.*
>
> *The original parallelogram- brick is divided as many chips of soul group. You were given yours. Lucky as it is like a disk to your memory - a great tool."*

Teresa was the first to confirm that Ramtha had been my father.

Will helped me navigate the journey with Ramtha. He was familiar with the territory. He was a student for many years of Carol Marron, a gifted spiritual teacher who led a group in Tucson, AZ. Before anyone heard of JZ Knight, Ramtha contacted Carol (who had been my sister in the Egyptian lifetime) and asked her to bring through the wisdom of Ramtha. She respectfully declined, preferring to lead her group in Tucson. Ramtha said he would have to go to his second choice even though he knew there would be problems.

Jewels

> *"In the Lemurian life, I was the one who became known as Lord Ameru. This was my first ascension in to full Christ Consciousness. I left Lemuria when it was sinking in to the ocean from volcanic activity, and took sacred objects, crystals, and scrolls to Lake Titicaca. There, another mystery school and spiritual community was begun, and it was an inter-galactic center as well, and a place where the Ascended Masters visited too, as teachers to the community over many thousands of years (like 33,000 years!)!!*
>
> *When I first became aware of the name Lord Meru, and also Ameru, I got 'a hit' on it and was very intrigued, wanting to know more. I figured that Lord Meru is an Ascended Master, but there is not much information about him that I have ever been able to find. One thing I did find was that he took sacred things form Lemuria*

to Lake Titicaca. I also became aware from another source in my research that there is a sacred etheric temple and community (like Shangri-La, but in a valley in the Andes). When I discovered this, it was another piece, in that I felt Lord Meru and Amaru founded that community long, long ago."

What I get for you Penny, was that as you were increasingly marginalized by the growing male dominance qualities of your father. You were at first confused and saddened, and you also were intuitively aware of whatever was 'not right', did not feel right. (Amaru helped you sort this out and educated you and validated you about what you were feeling and sensing within).

You turned more and more to your love of nature and beauty, creating 'gardens', first in your mind, then as holograms, and then materializing those holograms in to beautiful gardens for homes, (I spent 35 years as a landscape designer in this one) the temples, and the schools of that 'city' of Lemuria. JZ emulated her father, trying to be like him and to get his approval and notice in those ways, which were more masculine polarized. This was in a period of time where our androgyny had already been polarized into two genders for quite a while, and we were all exploring that, what was a 'descension' from our more light-body androgynous states of being in earlier Lemurian periods. This time period was much closer to the sinking of Lemuria, or the 'end' of Lemuria. The Ameru aspect of me was a mentor to you (one of them, but an important and close one), as I was 'older' and had been in the mystery schools and was in the midst of merging with Meru in the divine union - I should say - back in to the divine union! And Meru was also a friend and model for you of the balanced masculine who was one with the feminine divine being and expression. As you grew, you became a teacher of working with nature and the elementals, beauty and color and form, to create this kind of beauty in that culture at that time; and you entered in to a love partnership with someone who was a balanced, loving, and honoring masculine expression."

Channeled through Meline LaFont to Jewels from Buddha

"I greet you beloved one of my heart. I am your Master keeper and Buddha. I am here for you today to connect with you through spirit and to allow you a much deeper understanding of your current incarnation. As I am the Gatekeeper of this Planet and this Universe, I am allowed to step forward in your consciousness and to take you along a journey with me during this reading. Let us visit some places of old past memories so that such can be activated.

Many Earthly lifetimes ago in your past time-line called Lemuria, the land of MU, you have been in incarnation amongst many others. As you are now, the christed was embodied at that time and you were very advanced in your spiritual awakening such as a Goddess of Light is. You have had many different embodiments on Earth but this one was the grandest expansion for you and spiritual evolution one could have at these times.

Your christed Self is indeed a part/ fractal of the christed Magdalene, incarnated in your embodiment. You therefore carry parts of her being and consciousness and therefore you also share some past lives with her being of Light, which explains the bond felt within.

From all the former lives you have had, the Lemurian one, is the one whom has touched you and raised you the most in your being. Your christed embodiment at those times, had to let go of fear and un-purities as well as anger and frustrations in order to get to that point where you resided. You had reached such a pure refined energy and embodiment at that time that all that has happened over the years has affected you in so many ways of your being.

Your embodiment had to escape in order to be able and reside in such frequencies as you were lingering in as a consciousness. You have traveled around the world, looking for the perfect spot to reside and anchor your Lemurian priest energies of Light. Your embodiment was at that time the christed Amaru-Meru and into particular Lord Meru himself. This was your past incarnation where you carry a very big part of in this lifetime.

There is a strong connection with the Amaru-Meru through the embodiment of Lord Meru and so this explains your strength, your forces and power you carry inside of you! A beautiful Goddess of Light is residing inside of you and it is still asleep but very much awakening at this time, indeed, to say the least!

As this awakening journey continues to let you grow into the infinity that you are, a much deeper alignment with your soul level shall be felt and recognized, seen and known. You have it all inside of you, for there lies the key to infinity and beyond where all the Akashic records are stored and kept protected by us, the gatekeepers of Earth and this Universe. Amaru–Meru is your Goddess and Divine interaction on this Earthly plane that assists you through your current awakening at this time, reinforcing you, preparing you, allowing you and most of all reactivating you to the one that you ARE!

Your heart is a very big and clear space at this time, constantly lingering in the moment of Now, sharing and feeling the love that you are to so many other beloveds on this Earth. It is your mission and soul contract to bring the re-awakening into activation for this entire planet and Humanity, whomever is ready for it! As one of the Master Gatekeepers yourself, being this Divine goddess of Light, you shall now start to linger more in your own Divine reality of Light as it assists you in so many ways by residing in your heart space and work from and through that beloved space of yours.

You shall re-awaken so many beings in the upcoming times as your skills and knowledge come on-line for you again, and thus becomes accessible. Trust and be patience as the body copes with a great of deal right now, trying to find its growth through this denser reality. Give your

Earthly plane all the Love that you are from heart and invoke it with your beautiful Christed Light. Buddha

Jewels - Did I know Penny in this lifetime and what was Meru's possible connection with Ramtha?

"They were part of the same 'mystery school'. So, I did know the families of my cohort in the school as well. We lived in one of the 'centers' of living in Lemuria at that time, where the sacred schools were located.

As both Ramtha and myself were of the male gender, we bumped up against male polarity issues of competition, mistrust, anger, impatience - 'mirroring' each other's issues to move through them in to higher levels of consciousness and Being. One of the reasons we clashed was that Ramtha was descending in frequency and vibration at that time in Lemuria (pride, greed, jealousy, power, deceit) and I was ascending in to the Christ Consciousness - choosing to face all of my shadow aspects, including those being mirrored to me from others. This is a crucial step to becoming an ascended being. Meru was also merging with his divine feminine aspect in union, and Ramtha was polarizing more to the masculine. This was hard for his daughters!"

Shelly

"I do concur I was one of Ramtha's adopted children...I've felt/known/confirmed this before I met you. Did not realize it was from the Lemuria times. I am most happy to have met someone else from those times - you :)

Penny would walk among the paths and hurry along like no body's business handling all the important tasks she was assigned to. I hung back out of shyness and newness to the flock - wanting to help like she did but not having the tools to she possessed so easily."

I just realized - just like now - I want to help - but don't feel I possess the tools you so easily come to. I don't want to let you down, and struggle to catch-up."

Margaret –

"I never paid much attention to Ramtha because I was told in a previous spiritual activity that JZ Knight is channeling a False Hierarchy imposter. In pondering my connection to Ramtha (per Penny's chart) I did receive positive affirmation that I was another daughter of Ramtha on Lemuria 35,000 years ago. Surprise, surprise! So, Penny and I were sisters. I also received affirmation that Ramtha was an unascended master and is reincarnated as Babaji in the Himalayas, who is reputed to have been living in his current body for 5,000 years."

Joy –

"Penny and I were priestesses together in Lemuria. She was the senior priestess and I was an initiate. We had great pride in being positive role models for young girls and boys under our care as well. We loved Lemuria and its beautiful lands. We hated to leave when the disruption came but escaped and went to Atlantis where we again set up temples and mystery schools. It was a difficult transition as we lost so many loved one at the "end". Our hearts were so sorrowful, but we were grateful for our lives and a new beginning. Everything was lost but we had God and His guidance to start again. We both married and had children. Penny was a grandmother figure to my children. Life in Atlantis was good, and we thrived there. The technologies were so much more advanced than on Lemuria. We loved Atlantis but not as much as Lemuria, our first beautiful home. All is well now, and we brought with us Christ Consciousness and guidance to create a new God-centered place that could thrive and advance for so many years. We loved each other and worked together on so many projects and tasks. We became like mother and daughter, free to be ourselves and share our wisdom and knowledge with so many new beings. God's love was spread far and wide there for a long time. "

Jami –

"I have great love and feelings for Lemuria. I had several incarnations there serving mission. In one lifetime I was a temple initiate (I hear that it was at the temple of Isis) and many of my Magdalene sisters were also there at this time. We were trained and skilled and lived in peace and happiness, quietly doing our work. We were unexpectedly invaded by dark forces and split apart.

In another lifetime we knew the sinking of Lemuria was foreseen and could not be stopped. I left with a group of scientists and healers to "reseed" Atlantis with the wisdom and important sciences that were needed to keep alive and worked together there. The dark forces invaded us there as well and split me and my Lemurian husband (who is current a well-loved psychic in Sedona) up on opposite sides of the mission. I had a leadership role there and at one point had to make a horrific decision that chose the fate of who would immediately die at the hands of the dark force, and who would live a bit longer to try to further advance the mission.

When I moved to Sedona, I crossed paths with my long-lost Lemurian husband and deep remorse and grief came over me quickly and intensely. He supported me while all the grief, loss, and sad memories came up from those lifetimes. I was carrying a burden of feeling extraordinary failure and tremendous grief.

My next incarnations took me to Egypt for temple initiations there as we continued to try to do our work on this planet. Many of my current day Magdalene sisters from Sedona also incarnated into Egypt again. I find it amazing how we keep showing up for each other to share and contribute to the journey we are on."

Jayana- On the banks of the Danube

Ancient waters of the Danube
Flowing from antiquity forever
Never the same
Ever the One
I run, my sparkling head scarf
Flowing in the wind
I run into your welcoming arms, Mother.
Tears of joy wet our smiles
Like the Danube in the morning Sun.
"Mother, now I know it All.

It was Lemurian time. In bright sunlight I was running with a muslin red scarf dotted with golden sparkling stars and gold-embroidered border, floating behind me from my head in the breeze.

I saw this image several times passing by the Danube recently (July 2018). In it the mother figure is Penny. With tender smile on our lips and tears of joy hanging on our eye lash, we witness eternity, know it All.
No words....just awareness.

Nancy –

"It was a time of living in beauty. We were all there,

having a loving experience of perfect health,

Divine presence in each moment, in joy and

peace. This has been a lost memory.

This great wisdom ran through each of us then, that,

as we come together again in this lifetime, will be

ignited – not only individually, but as a whole,

to become a culture again, a people and bring

wonderful blessings to All."

Lessons from Lemuria...

35,000 years ago, we were the seers, healers, and holders of the chalice of Feminine Divinity. However, the seeds of failure were planted within us since we were unable to hold the energy in balance with the masculine. We are being asked to recognize the things that are holding us back from becoming our Divine selves again such as mistrust, judgements, and limiting beliefs about self-worth, self-punishment, and fear of harm if we exercise our divine abilities to create, heal, and speak our truth. We are worthy. We are the Divine Feminine pushing to be born in compliment to the Divine Masculine. It is time...

Lessons from Atlantis...

After the explosion and sinking of Lemuria, remnants of that world implanted and grew into the epoch known as Atlantis. The feminine was driven underground as the technology and dominance of the masculine strayed ever further from the balance of divine union. Galactic invasions implanted seeds of discord, distrust, and programs of greed, abandonment, hate, anger, self-punishment and betrayal within our DNA. The priestesses of Isis watched weeping, paralyzed, and helpless as that world imploded.

As **Alchemists of Light Working with the Field**, we are being asked to co-create a new world free from the burdens and missteps of past cultures. We have tools to learn from the collective including the Orions and Andromedins about the misuse of creative energy of the Masculine and Feminine. We are powerful beyond our own belief when we consciously work with the field (God) to co-create our reality.

In order to do this, we must shed the limiting beliefs, patterns, and impediments that are restricting this process. This may require doing soul-retrieval work to remove and nullify implants still in effect and clear healing patterns to return to our Divine state of Oneness.

No longer naïve, we are aware of the false-programming by "religions", curses, and outside influences that have kept us in denial and inert. By clearing our limited beliefs and impediments, we are raising our energetic vibration so that we elevate our inner vision into higher levels of awareness. Time to hold hands and move into this new world.

Nefertiti (c.1370 – c.1340 BC)

Nefereferauten Nefertiti was an Egyptian queen and the Great Royal Wife (chief consort) of Akhenaten, an Egyptian Pharaoh. Nefertiti and her husband were known for a religious revolution, in which they worshiped one god only, Aten, or the sun disc.

Akhenaten and Nefertiti were responsible for the creation of a whole new religion which changed the ways of worship within Egypt. With her husband, she reigned at what was arguably the wealthiest period of ancient Egyptian history. Some scholars believe that Nefertiti ruled briefly as Nefereferauten after her husband's death and before the accession of Tutankhamun, although this identification is a matter of on-going debate.

During the early years in Thebes Amenhotep IV had several temples erected at Karnack. One of the structures was dedicated to Nefertiti, In the fourth year of his reign, Amenhotep IV decided to move the capital to Akhenaten (modern Amara). In his fifth year he officially changed his name to Akhenaten and Nefertiti was henceforth known as Nefereferauten-Nefertiti. The name change was an indication of the ever-increasing importance of the cult of the Aten. It changed Egypt's religion from a polytheistic religion to a religion that may be better described as monolatry (the depiction of a single god as an object for worship) or henotheism (one god, who is not the only god).

During Akhenaten's reign Nefertiti enjoyed unprecedented power. By the twelfth year of his reign, there is evidence she may have been elevated to the status of co-regent, equal in status to the pharaoh.

Penny - *In 2007 I was visiting a friend and saw this image on the back of chairs he has just bought. I was stunned. I knew that I was this woman but did not know who she was. Years have passed, and I have come to understand who I was and the extraordinary time this was and the religious themes that were evolving into monotheism.*

I was told that I had been part of significant times in history and this was certainly one. Though it is now thought by some that Akhenaten went over the edge and was removed, perhaps by Nefertiti and her daughter Meritaten. The whole truth is still unfolding.

Channeled from Nefertiti through Penny Genter:

The sands of time are passing quickly, and it seems like just yesterday since we were part of the awakening taking place in Egypt. It was time to step above the imprint left by the star people and to begin an integration into a new vision of the world. Change is never easy as we found out. My husband was the first to sense the awareness of the shift that was taking place. Together we began something that, though short-lived, planted seeds of awareness in future generations. We were the guiding inspiration that began to turn the focus and the promise of Egypt.

The vast resources that were at our disposal allowed the building of edifices to higher authority but also to creating the infrastructure that would be needed for a modern economy. Unfortunately, the ego of Akhenaten got in the way. I was the first to realize this as things began to go astray. The secrets that were revealing themselves spoke to him and emboldened his lust for power and control of not only the earth, but the heavens as well. I saw this and, along with my daughter Meritaten, began laying the groundwork for assuming the throne in his place. Though there was karma to be played out for causing another's death, the consequences of following an out-of-control leader weighed heavily as well.

My reign in his stead was one of relative peace and prosperity until my son was able to come into his own power. Though the priestly class wrested back control and tried to obliterate what had been accomplished, the seeds of change were cast wide and the glory that was Egypt began to find root in other parts of the world. My face will ever be known for holding the loving cup of family together through the turmoil that frequently comes with change. Of all that is accomplished, it is the Love that survives in spite of apparent destruction. It is so...

Teresa -

"I remember Nefertiti's daughter, Meritaten.

As a child, a Nubian Slave (me) was given to her as a present at her 7th birthday, by her mother, Nefertiti. I became her favorite pet, went every place with her, carrying things for her. I dressed identical to my princess, I loved her so much.

In her training as the Secret Doctrines where given, I was allowed access to some of them. Thus, I learned somethings by being at ear's shot. I learned about the One God.

I died at al-Amar-Na, killed by soldiers of Amon Priesthood. By the obelisk."

Janice -

"I had many lifetimes during the Egyptian pyramid buildings and onward. In particular, I was a wife of the builder of the Djoser Step Pyramids (2686-2613BC). My husband then went to work one day, and I never got to say goodbye as he never returned (murdered).

In this lifetime he was Dr. Haing Ngor, who saved many of his Cambodian countrymen, he himself living through the Killing Fields, came to America and won the Academy Award for that movie and was murdered a few years later by opposing Pol Pot sympathizers here in America. I did not know why I cried and cried for months over Haing's death (I did not know him personally) but I was told."

Jami -

"This life line was huge for me. I started originally in the 80's having flash backs to this time-- buried alive, entombed, and working to "wrap" up other beings who weren't even dead but were wrapped to end their lives slowly as dictated from ones who then enslaved us to do this work. (Apparently people that were family to those that waring powers wanted dead. It was a common practice to kill the leader and take out the entire lineage with him by "wrapping them and entombing them with him"). Interesting that in this life, I spent many years working with funeral homes and hospice programs helping bring dignity, gentleness, love and compassion to individuals and families at death and transitions.

I have had multiple lives during the height of the powers of key Egyptian Dynasties. I remember being a temple initiate living with other young women and our temple was "stormed" by soldiers that caused much harm and fear to us. We were forced into slavery to support the "new" Pharaoh. I believe this was the life where I had to "wrap" those I loved and served and bury them alive after wrapping them. It was a horrible time for so many of us in this time line.

Yet, I also remember times of peace and sacredness, walking as a temple priestess among the golden streets of one of the kingdoms I served. I can still see, in my mind's eye, the glory of the Nile River and the lush lands that surrounded us at that time. Sometimes I can even smell the Nile River. I remember that many things that were happening at this time in history were related to an earth history that has been hidden and altered for modern day man. Much of what happened then seems to date back to other times in history and ancient civilizations that have been at war for a long time and started with origins beyond this planet.

I don't remember anything specific about knowing Nefertiti (Penny) at this time, but I do have flashbacks of walking the golden streets and a time of peace. However, I do remember the anxiety of living within the chaos of waring dynasties that disagreed over which Gods we would serve. I do feel I spent time over various life times at initiations within the Great Pyramid and visiting Egypt while I was living elsewhere.

I have recall of living at these times with some of my soul group, and I have had situations that came up for compassion and forgiveness multiple times.
One specific example was several years ago I lived with a woman who, in this lifetime, is a priestess with Mother Mary as her guide. Shortly after meeting her, I realized I had an Egyptian lifetime with this woman at the Hathor Temple of Isis and was her sister in a later Egyptian lifetime as well as her sister again in more modern-day lifetimes. In this one, she had a boyfriend who visited the household often. He had a volatile personality that was very dangerous at times. Because she believed he was her twin flame, she forgave him frequently for his abuse, putting the rest of the household in jeopardy because of his behaviors. (Author note -Remember, Twin Flames are not necessarily good partners!) *I had to finally evacuate the household to keep myself safe. I continued to be afraid for the life of my "temple sister" as I kept having premonitions of her demise if she continued allowing him in her life. I saw for myself, if I continued to be in any kind of connection with her, my life would be taken for "protesting" her.*

I consulted the angels, my Higher Self, and the Akashic records that showed me that these two had been in a karmic pattern for lifetimes and that I had been trying to rescue and protect my friend from him for several lifetimes, only to watch her life gruesomely end and meet my own demise, trying to protect and help her.

The records revealed to me an incident where dark forces violently invaded those of us that served at the Hathor Temple of Isis. I discovered that we were all manipulated and implanted to mistrust and turn against each other. This being who had once had a great love for my friend became slammed with dark forces and implanted with seeds of destruction that were continuing to play out. I had help clearing the anxiety and fear from my memory and was able to rescue and integrate the aspect of my soul still in trauma from that timeline. I spent almost two years actively praying and directing healing energies to heal and transmute the darkness involved for all of us involved in this timeline. Many of us in Sedona, along with Lightworkers in Colorado, were collectively doing this healing work together.

With understanding, I was ultimately able to have compassion and choose forgiveness and unconditional love for everyone involved. I no longer am afraid or charged energy about this time in history, but a healthy respect and compassion for all that we lived. Many Lightworkers have worked to clear intense dark energies from intense timelines like this in history, yet people involved in karmas in these periods of time have to still do their own work to stop a karmic pattern and find their heart's way to forgiveness and resolution."

Michael – I "get" that Michael was Akhenaten in that lifetime. Today he is a spiritual teacher that shares insights about God and the path of Christ Consciousness.

Jeri – Soul sister in this and other lifetimes was Meritan in that one and has written about it in her book ***Return of the Goddess – the Hidden History of Nefertiti, Akhenaten, Mary Magdalene and Scotia.***

Cleopatra (69BC – 30BC)

Cleopatra VII Philopater was the last active pharaoh of Ptolemaic Egypt. A member of the Ptolemaic dynasty, a family of Macedonian Greek speaking origin that ruled Egypt after Alexander the Great's death during the Hellenistic period. Cleopatra did learn to speak Egyptian and represented herself as the reincarnation of the Egyptian goddess Isis.

Cleopatra originally ruled jointly with her father and later with her brothers who she married per Egyptian custom but eventually became the sole ruler. As pharaoh she consummated a liaison with Julius Caesar that solidified her grip on the throne.

After Caesar's assassination in 44 BC she aligned with Mark Anthony in opposition to Caesar's legal heir, Octavian. With Anthony she bore twins and another son. After losing the Battle of Actinium to Octavian's forces, Anthony committed suicide. Cleopatra followed suit, according to tradition by means of an asp bite.

Her legacy survives in numerous works of art and many dramatizations of incidents from her life in literature.

Channeled from Cleopatra through Penny Genter,

Strong women have to prove themselves in every arena of their life. As Pharaoh I was the supreme authority in my time but with big power comes big responsibility. It is easy to judge previous generations by standards of the present but that is unfair. Things like marriage among siblings, though it has present day taboos, was something that was desired and expected in the world in which I lived in order to insure bloodlines. Unfortunately, my dynastic marriages were doomed to failure and I had to look elsewhere in order to produce progeny.

The life of a ruler is never their own. At the root of every decision is the affect it will have on the country they rule. Alliances between nations are frequently consummated in the bedchambers of rulers of their respected nations. The alliances I made with Rome may have begun as such but eventually became the meeting of twin souls in a match that had divine origins.

I was blessed with a demeanor that allowed the secrets of Isis to be revealed in the passions of my body which not only opened to my lovers but produced the offspring necessary to insure the dynastic lineage that was required by my status as Pharaoh. It was one of the more pleasant obligations of my post.

As supreme commander, I let my passions and my heart interfere with my judgement in military matters. Empathy is not always not the best attribute if one is to succeed in the masculine mode of commander-in-chief; at least not in that time and place. Though I realized my defeat and choose to exit that lifetime ahead of schedule, I nevertheless left vivid images that would be replayed for future generations of a ruler who lustily ruled from her heart as well as her head. And so, it is...

Penny – *I have always been drawn to the story and the image of Cleopatra but knew not why. Costume or "Come as you were" parties, I was drawn to dressing as Cleopatra.*

All my life I have been told that I look like Elizabeth Taylor. I believe we are different rays of the same soul that was Cleopatra and reincarnated in this lifetime. In this lifetime Elizabeth chose the red ray, and I the indigo ray. Red tends to mean very passionate and physical, while indigo is intuitive and psychic.

Vicky – I lived many lifetimes in Egypt and this is the one I remember with you.

We were priestesses in court where we were doing offerings and preparing medicine.
Our words were heard and respected.
We had the queen's ears and helped her make decisions.
We were able to travel in the shadows and bring knowledge from the other side where humans could not.
The herbs we grew were very secrete and we passed knowledge only by teaching.
We were from the bloodline and connected with the royal family.
We remembered, and we were aware of the special work we had come on earth to share with humans.
*We did infusion of oil and flowers. (*Author's note – Interesting *that* in this lifetime I produced flower essences with essential oils for many years*)*
We could modify energy with sound which was part of our DNA.
We were aware of astronomy and physics.
We had multiple human bodies living at the same time.
Also, I wanted to share when we were the children of the sun and how powerful and magical it was at that time.

I have to say I am actually pretty impressed with what I wrote. It resonates so much.
I closed my eyes and was like a movie.

Joy –

"I worked in the temple with Penny during Cleopatra's reign. We were colleagues who also were goddesses/priestesses. We were close to Cleopatra and taught her all we knew of the mysteries and God's love. We started temples in Egypt and kept God's love alive in this culture. Our role was to be support for Cleopatra and educate her in "the mysteries".

Mary Jacobe Cleopas (23BC – 40AD)

In 1995 I went to a bookstore, looking for a book to "fall into my hands". One did on channeling. I thought "Oh that would be fun", little realizing the profound effect it would have on my life.

I did everything she said, sat down with my tape recorder, opened my mouth but nothing came out! Then I remembered that Ruth Montgomery had done this on her typewriter, so I sat down at my computer, went into a meditative state, placed my hands on the keys and closed my eyes. Mother Mary came through, word by word, phrase by phrase. It was beautiful, loving and far more eloquent than anything I could write so I knew it was not from me. We have been doing this for over 20 years and written several books together.

Through the years I have become aware of our connection that goes back to our time together at the time of Jesus and before. In the Jesus lifetime, I was her niece, Mary, daughter of Jacob and eventually wife of Cleopas. I was four years older and there at her birth. We grew up together in the Essene community at Qum Run and raised our families together. Two of my sons and one stepson were apostles. Edgar Casey tells about when I was healed by Jesus. I was one of the Mary's at the crucifixion and went with the family to Egypt and then France.

In 2008 a friend who had been Mary Salome in that lifetime and I went on a spirit-guided trip to France, in the steps of Mary Magdalene. Entering the church of Mary Magdalene in Saintes Marie-de-la-Mer were confronted with an effigy of a small boat containing Mary Jacobe and Mary Salome. Our bones are venerated in the church.

This connection to the time and the soul group has been very strong. Not only do the people in the soul group continue to show up, but we seem to be exploring ways to carry on what we learned in that lifetime. Many of us are ministers, chaplains, rabbis, and spiritual presenters of teachings and understandings that adhere more closely to the words and message of Jesus, rather than the interpretations of present religious institutions.

In 2014 Mother Mary Anna asked me to put together a book and classes on *Creating Sacred Relationship*s and ***Hieros Gamos – the Sacred Union of the Divine Feminine and Divine Masculine,*** which I did. In the introduction she said:

"Many years have passed since we strode the dusty paths of Galilee together. It is time for the things that we knew to be true to be shared with the world. It pleasures me to know that despite the passage of time and experience, we still are able to connect so readily at the level of the heart. Your wisdom now, as ever, transcends experience and connects with a higher source. Mary Anna"

I continue to value her wisdom above all others because it is so couched in love.

As Jesus had his twelve apostles, Mary Magdalene also had twelve women apostles. We have come together as twelve sisters in this time period to heal wounds from that time and continue our mission together.

We all carried wounds and impediments including pain, grief, sadness as well as anger at the way we saw things happening. Many could not understand why He choose the path he did and didn't do things differently. Many Essenes felt Jesus had abandoned them. We were blinded by our love for the man and his message. Many choose to deny or curse God for allowing what we believed to be a travesty to take place because we did not see the bigger picture.

The collective amnesia and emotional blocks we carry from that lifetime are barriers to our healing and vibrational growth. We are working together to remove the emotional impingements in our cellular memory from that lifetime and replace it with the opposite energy. Vows of not allowing forgiveness of ourselves and others, feelings of lack of power, and abandonment are being renounced so that we can move forward once again in service together.

Teresa – *with Mary, Mother of Jeshua, the Christ,*

I was younger by few years. I received Temple Training with her as one of the Virgins.

As I was not taken out, I trained in the Essene ways, as a seer. I was unhappy there as it was a restricted life (convent like).

As I grew older I trained the younger ones.

From the terrace of the Temple I saw Mary and her friends including you.

I died at around 25

Amara – I "get" that Amara was **Mary Salome**, wife of Zebedee and mother of apostles

James and John. We were among those that traveled with the family to Gaul (France) in the rudderless boat, landing in Saintes Maries-de-la-Mer. We were drawn back there in 2008.

Janice *During Jesus' lifetime, I was his grandmother,* ***Anna*** *(sometimes called Hanna). I was his teacher while his mother, Mary raised other children."*

I "get" that she was also **Joseph of Arimathea**, Anna's son.

Azura – I "get" that Azura was also Anna**.**

(Author' note – remember, many people can host an "aspect" of the same soul from a previous lifetime. Since the Akashic memories are carried in the DNA, many carry the DNA and therefore the cellular memory of that lifetime.)

Bo – I "get" that Bo was **John,** son of Zebedee (nicknamed with his brother, Sons of Thunder). He was the youngest and beloved by Jesus Christ; A fisherman by trade with Andrew; The Zebedee family was wealthy. Brother of James.

I "get" that he was also **Nicodeamus**, the disciple of Jesus who is said to have carved the *Volto Santo di Lucca*, the face of Jesus in Lucca, Italy. Nicodemus was a Pharisee and a member of the Sanhedrin mentioned in the Gospel of John, most notable for assisting Joseph of Arimathea in the burial of Jesus. In this lifetime Bo is a sometimes chainsaw artist.

Jewels- I "get" that Jewels was the **centurion** mentioned in Matthew 8:5-13. A number of Roman centurions are mentioned in the New Testament, including one who came to Jesus for help when his servant was paralyzed and in pain. That man's faith in Christ was so strong that Jesus healed the servant from a great distance.

"You are correct Penny, though I was not aware of that before. I see now that I was serving as a bridge between cultures and as a link from The Christ's work to the group soul of Rome. (All of these things play out in time, through time: the service work we all do for a much bigger picture, and the soul agreements we make with our soul groups: especially in a major shift of the ages, as this visit from The Christ was at that time.)

As one of the 144,000 aspects of The Christ-Magdalene Oversoul or Monad, I was also a fractal part of both The Christ and The Magdalene (in support on inner levels), after the point when Jesus was Overlighted by Lord Maitreya and became the full embodiment of The Christ as a planetary, galactic, universal and cosmic 'office'; and as the head of the Planetary Hierarchy - The Masters of Wisdom, are the Heart Center of our planet. Many of the 144,000 aspects were very much supporting and assisting, as One with The Christ-Magdalene, in their mission in Palestine. Once again, we are all in this together!"

Will – I "get" that Will was **Philip Nathaniel Bartholomew,** analytical disciple, sincere and royal background.

Kathleen - I "get" that Kathleen carries the cellular memory of **Mary Magdalene**.

Jami - I "get" that Jami was a cousin of Jesus.

"Penny, we traveled many circles together-- before, during and after the time of Christ. Meeting you and participating in many of the Magdalene Circles and the events and gatherings you would host awoke many memories within me of the earlier times we have all shared together within our soul family. I am part of the Essence lineage that prepared the way for Christ as well as carried on with the work after his time. These memories awoke in me after I moved to Sedona and met many people familiar to me from our soul group.

I have memory of being a "healer" who helped Jesus, along with many others who had been trained to do "transmuting" work, at the actual Crucifixion. We were assisting with what we were taught in the earlier temples as well as in the schools of our time, "transmuting." (It took many life times to learn this). It took many of us to help open the Ascension portal that Christ focused on with his time at the cross. He focused on his direct ascension and many of us helped as "defensive ends," working with and transmuting energies that wanted to block or alter his success at this. We were all working for the sake of humanity to ensure that portal of Christ Frequencies would open safely as it was destined to be with his participation in this rite. And we were destined to help, and then go into hiding and maintain the path.

I have had some trauma and healing to love into since the time of Christ, as I seemed to have not realized the time it would take to achieve complete success of this Christ Light Portal on our plane, and I learned to blame myself that I hadn't done enough to help things move faster for humanity. I have had life times of persecution and being diminished because of what we knew and the threat we were to establishment that wanted to control the people. I had hoped to uphold the Divine Feminine Truth with greater ease, yet the hardships and pain of what seemed "a world gone mad" took its toll on me and I limped my way into victimization and died a broken heart many times since.

Since meeting you, Penny, so many pieces have come together. I was able to meet more and more people of our soul group and remember the greater mission. Gratefully, books would fall into my life at the right time to help me pick up lost or dropped threads of the wisdom I was starved to remember. I was able to quench my thirst for awakening to some of the wisdom I had once known through so many times in ancient goddess temples, schools of initiation and even with direct teachings from Mother Mary and Mary Magdalene. In one way or another, I had been looking my whole life for these "lost teachings," looking for and studying the mysteries from a young age, including being a very frustrating child to the local priests I grew up with who told me I should have faith rather than ask so many inappropriate questions!

I have also seen within our soul group that we have danced in many roles together through time, learning and evolving from any experiences together. You have been a great reminder to me, Penny, of Hieros Gamos and the path of balance and honor for our Divine Feminine and our Divine Masculine. Until these teachings you helped remind me of and mirrored to me, I was lost in the imbalance of alienation that comes from despair of feeling broken and weakened by the programs and confusion that created disconnect within our hearts that once so fully knew Love. I realized we have all played every part in which the greater of ourselves could learn and blossom forward. I began to forgive myself for the difficult roles I have played, for that which I thought I forgot, and that which thought I could have done it any better. Through the teachers and inspirations that came to me though many of the Magdalene gatherings you hosted, I learned a gentler way to love and connect with my heart into the sacred chamber with Christ love. "

Kevin – I "get that he was **Judas Iscariot**. He talks about this in his book, ***Trust, Patience, Surrender***.

Gordon, **Harry,** and Jim – I "get" that Gordon, Harry, and Jim all carry the cellular memory of my stepson by Alpheus, the **Apostle Matthew (Levi),** the tax collector. Gordon was a CPA in this lifetime

Susan **-** I "get" that you have DNA from both Jesus and Mary Magdalene because you were their daughter Sah'r.

> *"Oh Penny!! My name of origin is Sahr Nitzia... I've known that for 4 yrs. now. Wow!! Confirmed."*

Margaret **–**

> *"When I first heard a lecture about the book Jesus Lived in India, I felt a very strong connection to India and the truth of them being there. I didn't know I was related to Yeshua until Penny showed me her chart where I was sister-in-law to Yeshua. But it made sense because I have always felt Yeshua as a beloved brother and not a "Lord" to be worshipped. On the other hand, I did not feel a connection to Palestine or a desire to go there. I have felt a life-long connection to India and visited there in 2008.*
>
> *A daughter of mine in that India lifetime is my favorite niece today. When I held her in my arms shortly after her birth, I felt the spiritual connection with her, as in "cosmic tingles" all over my body. At the time, however, I did not know the significance of this. Only many years later did it make itself known.*
>
> *A dear friend I'm close to here in Arizona was a son in that same life in India."*

Harmony –

> *"What rings true for me is that I was Judy, first Essene High Priestess in a male dominated society. My parents dedicated me to the Temple before I was born - not yet knowing that I was female. I studied at the mystery schools in Alexandria and became initiated at the Temple of the Sphinx. Later on, I became the head teacher of all the children of Israel, including Yeshua. I traveled with him on some of his journeys to other countries such as India and Egypt.*
>
> *I remember watching Yeshua being spat upon and then crucified - which broke my heart... I also have memories of a mass exodus, where we were hiding out in caves. I may have had two lives during that time."*

Michael – I "get" that Michael was Mariam, adopted sister of Jesus.

Debra –

"I feel I was an Essene. I have always loved the sight of vineyards. I saw vineyards, gathering grapes, assisting. I was young. I asked if I had known Jesus then – Yes!

I knew you in that lifetime. I was a child when Jesus was alive then, in the Essene community. We played together as children but did not gather grapes together. I was a niece of Jesus', daughter of Miriam. I was a little older than you.

Nancy – I "get" that Nancy was a priestess in the Isis temples who trained with Mary Magdalene.

"In the Holy Land when Jesus and Mary Magdalene
were the main focus of our lives, it was a time of
great joy, and then a time of intense sadness. Those
who were there have been trying to bring this deep
love back, this Divine wisdom that carried each of us
into our own holiness.
We each played a part and carry a piece from this
lifetime, what we brought to the wholeness, as
whole beings. The question is:
Who are we now and what are we doing? Which part
of this memory do we each carry? Will reclaiming the
wisdom of Mary Magdalene help us embrace this
deep memory? Do you know what your part is now?"

Joy –

"I knew Penny in my lifetime with Jesus and Mary Magdalene as a "sister" in blood and marriage. We spent a lot of time together and did healings in temples and in neighboring villages. We lived together at times between moves in France and Israel. We also taught young girls and initiated them into mystery schools and rites.

We loved helping the young girls and helping women give birth and healing villagers.

We also spent a lot of time with Jesus and Mary Magdalene in their travels and teachings. We supported them, especially Mary Magdalene in France and helped her set up churches in various places. We loved Mary and Jesus so much and tried to do our best to help them and keep their families safe.

I took care of young Penny after she was born and taught her the ways of the priestess. She grew up with the Essenes and became a beautiful young girl and woman. We had a wonderful lifetime with Mary and Jesus, even though it also involved a lot of fear for our lives and the lives of our loved ones. We had a lot of fulfillment in achieving what we had come to do in that lifetime."

John –

I "get" that John was my father Jacob, brother of Joseph and therefore uncle of Jesus. I also "get" that he reincarnated as John Mark, the writer of the Second Gospel who documented the teachings of Simon Peter.

Titus Flavius Josephus (37 – c.100 AD)

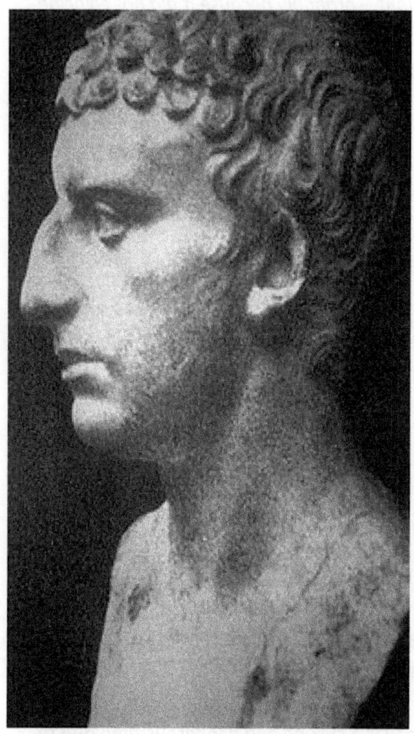

Titus Flavius Josephus, born Joseph ben Matityahu, was a first-century Romano-Jewish scholar, historian and hagiographer, who was born in Jerusalem—then part of Roman Judea—to a father of priestly descent and a mother who claimed royal ancestry.

Flavius Josephus fully defected to the Roman side and was granted Roman citizenship. He became an advisor and friend of Vespasian's son Titus, serving as his translator when Titus led the Siege of Jerusalem, which resulted—when the Jewish revolt did not surrender—in the city's destruction and the looting and destruction of Herod's Temple (Second Temple).

Josephus recorded Jewish history, with special emphasis on the first century CE and the First Jewish–Roman War, including the Siege of Masada. His most important works were ***The Jewish War*** (c. 75) and ***Antiquities of the Jews*** (c. 94). ***The Jewish War*** recounts the Jewish revolt against Roman occupation (66–70). *Antiquities of the Jews* recounts the history of the world from a Jewish perspective for an ostensibly Roman audience. These works provide valuable insight into first century Judaism and the background of Early Christianity.

The extant manuscripts of the writings of the 1st-century Romano-Jewish historian, Flavius Josephus include references to Jesus and the origins of Christianity. *Josephus' Antiquities of the Jews*, written around 93–94 AD (nearly 25 years after the first known Gospel, Mark, dated around 70 AD), includes two references to the biblical Jesus Christ and a reference to John the Baptist.

The works of Josephus provide crucial information about the First Jewish-Roman War and also represent important literary source material for understanding the context of the Dead Sea Scrolls and late Temple Judaism.

Penny –

I can only assume that my interest in seeing the larger patterns of history and experience have roots in this earlier incarnation as Josephus. Interestingly enough, growing up I had little interest in the "history" I was being taught – probably because it did not coincide with the truth as I remembered it. History is indeed recorded by the survivors, not by the combatants.

Teresa - *Again Essene.*

I was born at the Masada site, as male. I died during the siege.

So, in both lifetimes I had a brief encounter with you, in the background because of our beliefs, and community.

Bo – I "get" that Bo was an Essene and the wife of Teresa. They both perished in the siege of Masada.

Janice - I "get" that Janice was a Roman soldier at the siege of Masada.

Dave – I "get" that Dave was **Merilius**, Roman Prefect (leader of an administrative area) of Judea AD 38-41 under Caligula, AD 37 – 41. He was the seventh governor of this province. He was appointed by the emperor following the recall of Pontius Pilate and the temporary oversight of Marcellus. The period of his prefecture was a stirring and dangerous time due to Caligula's determination to turn the temple at Jerusalem into an imperial shrine with an enormous statue of himself in the guise of Jupiter and the Jews equal determination to accept no such thing, but nothing is recorded of Marcellus' part because the important decisions and negotiations were necessarily taken over by The Syrian Governor (Legate) Publius Petronius.

With the statue being constructed in Sidon and two legions of Roman troops waiting on the border of Galilee to enforce the imperial order, war was eventually avoided by the intervention of Agrippa who dissuaded his friend from such provocation. Soon afterwards Caligula was assassinated, and Agrippa was appointed to take Marcellus' place, but with the appellation of "king."

Kevin – I "get" that Kevin was Marcellus' wife.

Lanna – I "get" that Lanna assisted me in the recording of history.

Jeff and I spent many hours in this lifetime on the couch watching the Masterpiece Theatre series *I Claudius* that undoubtedly brought up remembrance of our lives in ancient Rome. I believe he was one of my assistants in the recording of history.

Percival, Merlin's Apprentice (610 AD)

Nikolai Tolstoy hypothesized that Merlin is based on a historical personage, probably a 6th-century Druid living in southern Scotland. His argument is based on the fact that early references to Merlin describe him as possessing characteristics which modern scholarship (but not that of the time the sources were written) would recognize as Druidical - the inference being that those characteristics were not invented by the early chroniclers but belonged to a real person.

According to Breton legend, the legendary wise man Merlin climbed the Pine of Brenton just as shamans climb the World Tree. Here, he had a profound revelation and he never returned to the mortal world. In later versions, Merlin's *glas tann* was mistranslated as a "glass house". and from these words the name of Glastonbury, in Somerset, England previously known as Avalon.

Robert de Boron lays great emphasis on Merlin's power to shapeshift, on his joking personality, and on his connection to the Holy Grail. *Merlin*. It was originally attached to a cycle of prose versions of Robert's poems, which tells the story of the Holy Grail: brought from the Middle East to Britain by followers of Joseph of Arimathea, the Grail is eventually recovered by Arthur's knight Percival.

In Robert de Boron's account *Saint Graal*, **Percival** is of noble birth; His mother is usually unnamed but plays a significant role in the stories. His sister is the bearer of the Holy Grail; After the death of his father, Perceval's mother takes him to the forests where she raises him ignorant to the ways of men until the age of 15. Eventually, however, a group of knights passes through his wood, and Perceval is struck by their heroic bearing. Wanting to be a knight himself, the boy leaves home to travel to King Arthur's court. After proving his worthiness as a warrior, he is knighted and invited to join the Knights of the Round Table.

The **Round Table** is King Arthur's famed table in the Arthurian legend, around which he and his Knights congregate. As its name suggests, it has no head, implying that everyone who sits there has equal status. The Round Table takes on new dimensions in the romances of the late 12th and early 13th century, where it becomes a symbol of the famed order of chivalry which flourishes under Arthur. In Robert de Boron's *Merlin*, written around the 1190s, the wizard Merlin creates the Round Table in imitation of the table of the Last Supper and of Joseph of Arimathea's Holy Grail table. This table, here made for Arthur's father Uther Pendragon rather than Arthur himself, has twelve seats and one empty place to mark the betrayal of Judas. This seat must remain empty until the coming of the knight who will achieve the Grail. The Didot *Perceval*, a prose continuation of Robert's work, takes up the story, and the knight Percival sits in the seat and initiates the Grail quest.

On the BBC television series Merlin, Percival is a large, strong commoner. After helping to free Camelot from the occupation of Morgana, Morgause, and their immortal army (which is supplied by a grail-like goblet called the Cup of Life), he is knighted along with Lancelot, Elyan and Gwaine, against the common practice that knights are only of noble birth. He is also one of the few Round Table knights to survive Arthur's death.

Penny –

My journey with Merlin in this lifetime began in 1996 when I began receiving channelings from Merlin, Mother Mary and Quan Yin that I included in my book, ***Returning Home – A Workbook for Ascension.***

I was drawn back to England then to Scotland where we attended an international Flower Essence Conference at ***Findhorn*** *that reawakened much of the Druidic knowledge I had learned in that lifetime.*

I had immersed myself since 1973 in horticulture and was putting the pieces together as I began to converse with nature spirits in designing landscapes and preparing flower essences. I remember the first book I read by Machaelle Small Wright on Gardening with Nature Intelligences. I was blown away. It reawakened a deep knowing that this is something that I must do, though I knew not why.

I learned kinesiology and began to converse with the devas and nature spirits of the plants and created unique remedies for many of the dysfunctions of our time. For ten years we operated a flower essence company that made these available to those with ears to hear. Merlin continued to guide me to create the "magical", or so it seemed because it was outside the norm of other's knowledge.

We built a geodesic adobe in the mountains of New Mexico with a Chartres pattern labyrinth, a mandala shaped community garden where we shared our life with others on the path. Our enchanted home in the mountains was a refuge and sanctuary for the fairies, nature spirits, and elementals that helped co-create our life and our essences until my husband's death.

I am still drawn to the round table where all are equally important and co-create something that honors all. I facilitate women's circles and host meals around large round tables that foster equal participation and sharing. It is the pattern of love and community made manifest.

Teresa - *During the Life of King Arthur*

"I was born a peasant, working at farming fields.
I took fresh vegetables to the kitchen of the King at Camelot and stayed for a while tending horses and as a stable care giver.

I kept low profile as the family had strong Druid Connections that used Stonehenge, as a Portal to cross Galactic ways and Planes of Dimensions. Very few people were aware of this.
I used to guide important people of the court.
It seems I am always working behind scenes.
Percival was a good sponsor."

Don - I "get" that Don was one of the Knights of the Round Table.

Janice -

*You were Percival in King Arthur's time. I was **Arthur Pendragon**, and I was surprised to find out from Ashtar (Channeled by Terrie Cunningham Symons) that I was also **Guinevere.** Apparently, we can "be" our twin flame also in the same lifetime, and he said that I am, once again, my own twin flame. Perhaps that is why I can relate to both male and female sides of me (aha, the Gemini). When I was younger I could go into this lifetime very easily and see myself with armor and sword...the battle horses, the tents. I was always reading the Classic Comic books of Arthur as well. In this lifetime, I have related to the "warrior" in me and was born into a military family but since I was a female, I was on the "supporting the troops side" (wife/daughter/sister). I finally laid to rest my penchant for war & have adopted the dove symbol of peace. I do have to laugh that I had adopted a rescue Scotty dog in this lifetime and promptly named him Merlin."*

Jeff I "get" that Jeff was Percival's mother

Michael – I "get" that Michael was **Merlin.**

John –

I "get" that John was "The Lady of the Lake". The **Lady of the Lake** is an enchantress in the Matter of Britain, , the body of medieval literature and legend associated with King Arthur. She plays a pivotal role in many stories, including giving Arthur his sword Excalibur, enchanting Merlin, and raising Lancelot after the death of his father.

John has a profound connection to Avalon in this lifetime.

Jami –

I am told that I was an aspect of Guenivere's sister. We were raised together in community and were schooled on many things most girls were not privy to. We treated each other like sisters. When she served King Arthur's Queen, I was on her "Council of advisory. Guenivere relied on the collective wisdom of her most trustworthy women allies as she found each woman had valuable insights to help her feel best prepared to make difficult decisions and recommendations. King Arthur valued and relied on Guenivere's intuitions, insights and recommendations. After his death, Guenivere brought her women's council to the round table and the knights accepted and respected the women. I was married to one of King Author's knights, although he did not serve at the round table.

I have seen flashes of something that indicates to me that after Guenivere died, the kingdom wasn't told at first. The council continued to serve as "The voice of Guenivere" so that our position could remain "strong" to our allies and enemies. The people were told that Guenivere had a contagious sickness and was behind closed doors until she healed. That bought us time without the kingdom being alarmed to decide what to do next. The outcome was not successful. My memory is blocked beyond this, but it feels like we were "absorbed" into another kingdom and at their mercy, which wasn't attentive.

Li Qingzhao (1084-1151 AD)

Li Qingzhao was a Chinese poetry writer and poet of the Song dynasty. The Song dynasty restored unity and made Song China the richest, most skilled and most populous countries on earth. The Southern Song capital was at Linan (now Hangzhou). Social life during the Song was very vibrant. Citizens gathered to view and trade precious art works. Technology, science, philosophy, mathematics, and engineering flourished over the course of the Song. Confucianism was reinvigorated and infused with Buddhist ideals.

She was born into a family of scholar-officials. Her father was a student of Su Shi. He had a large collection of books and Li was educated during her childhood. She was unusually outgoing and knowledgeable for a woman of noble birth.

Before she got married, her poetry was already well known within elite circles. In 1101 she married Zhao Mincheng, with whom she shared interests in art collecting and epigraphy (inscription collecting). They lived in present-day Shandong. They were not particularly rich but shared enjoyment of collecting inscriptions and calligraphy. They collected many books along with a love of poetry and often wrote poems for each other.

Fighting took place in Shandong and their house was burned. The couple took many of their possessions and fled to Nanjing where they lived for a year. Zhao died in 1129 on the way to an official post. The death of her husband was a cruel stroke from which Li never recovered. Her early poetry describes the carefree days as a woman of high society and is marked by its elegance.

Penny –

I have always had a respect and love for Chinese culture. I was able to travel throughout China in 1988, including Hangzhou where Li had been. I had many Chinese furnishings in my home and enjoy cooking Chinese dishes.

Certainly, my love and interest in art and literature is a common theme of many of my lifetimes.

In 2003 I had my first bunion surgery to correct deformities in my feet. Following a second surgery in 2007, I had a sound healer/psychic who connected with my mother in that lifetime. She apologized for having my feet bound which caused the deformities that I carry in my cellular memory but explained that that is what was required of women of noble birth in that lifetime.

I recently had a woman who specializes in removing past-life trauma from cellular memory tell me that she does this, and it does not require the surgery. Timing is everything in life!

Teresa

I was humble and trained very young to be a Taoist Nun.

I was skilled in Calligraphy. Li used to come looking for art, and calligraphy Art at our Temple.

We had a Buddha Temple for retreats, where sometimes she came to meditate.

Cathar at Montsegur (1244 AD) (France)

"Cathars grew in influence in the Languedoc throughout the twelfth century. Catholic chroniclers record that Cathars had become the majority religion in many places, and that Catholic churches were abandoned and in ruin. Of the Catholic clergy that remained some, perhaps most, were themselves Cathar believers. The Papacy responded initially by instigating preaching campaigns and engaging in public debates, both of which proved humiliating failures for the crack teams of theologians sent by the Pope.

The next response, in 1208, was a war, or more accurately a series of wars. Modern writers refer to them as the Cathar Wars, but traditionally the series was referred to as the ***Albigensian Crusade****. It was a formal crusade in the full sense of the word - preached and directed by the papacy and offering participants the remission of sins and an assured place in heaven. The Crusaders regarded themselves as being "on God's business" and referred to themselves as "pilgrims". Like all crusades it was a war, declared by the Pope, (Innocent III) backed by the Roman Church with promises of remission of sins and a guaranteed place in heaven.*

From the first major siege (at Beziers) in 1209 the War became one of French (+ their allies) against the independent people of the Languedoc (+ their allies). Instead of Catholics against Cathars it was, up until 1242 at least, consistently Catholics on one side against Cathars and

Catholics defending the Cathars on the other. Terror tactics included mass indiscriminate slaughter, various atrocities, and mass burnings as at Montsegur.

On March 16 in the year 1244, beneath the imposing edifice of Montsegur, the defenders of the Cathars and approximately 200 of the remaining Cathar parfait (perfecti), marched out in file where they were rounded up on a great field, fenced around and piled high with dry tinder and branches, and there burned to their deaths.

Cathars seem to be a branch of the earlier Manichaean dispensation, having inherited their traditions from the Bogomil sect of Christianity, who themselves inherited the Manichaean dispensation when it came to Bulgaria. From Bulgaria the Bogomils spread the religion of the Cathars to some parts of Italy, Northern Spain and Southern France, where they were called Cathars (Pure Ones) or the Bons Hommes (the Kind or Good People). In typical Gnostic fashion they eschewed the dogma, rules, regulations, indulgences, and penances of the mainstream Roman Catholic Church. For them a knowledge of a higher love and a practice of human kindness was what was spiritually and effectually necessary. "A new commandment I give unto you: that you love God with all your heart and soul and mind, and that you love your neighbor as yourself." (The Gospel according to St. John).

The most well-known group of Gnostics to emerge were the Cathars. They were very passive, peaceful, and highly critical of the Catholic Church and its corruption. The Cathars were a group of holy men and women who embraced a life of reunification, spirituality, and simplicity. They called themselves the "Good Christians". They represented honesty and truth.

Like the Manichaeans and Buddhists their attitude toward the world may be better described as that of compassion. They did not find value in accumulating hordes of wealth, yet they retained what was necessary to see after their own welfare and those of others. They were one of the first religions to organize hospice work and education among the poor. St. Francis' emphasis on poverty and his reverence of nature in his Hymn of the Creatures, as a reminder of the Light of God behind the creation, may have been inspired by Cathar teachings.

They held a distinction between the initiated Knowers (Perfecti) and the uninitiated and faithful Believers (Credenti). They celebrated a communal meal in a sacramental fashion, recited the Lord's Prayer as a sacrament and were particularly known for their practice of the sacramental rite of the Consolamentum. They were anti-hierarchical primarily in the political and social sphere. They combined both nobility and peasantry and treated each other from whatever social class as brother or sister. Unlike the catholic church there was no male dominance in this movement.

They were not anti-ritualists; they opposed the Catholic sacraments in response to the increasing materialism of the Roman Catholic Church, its practice of unconsciously performed rituals and the equally unconscious leaders within the mainstream Church. The Roman Catholic Church of their time had begun to reduce everything to the physical exteriorized form without consciousness of the spiritual intent or purpose. Because of their popularity, the Cathars eventually became a threat to the power and authority of the Roman Catholic Church.

The crusade against the Cathars, however, was primarily a political rather than a religious one. King Phillippe Auguste of France wanted the rich lands and wealth of Southern France, so he joined with the Pope (Pope Innocent III) to declare a religious crusade against them. The Albigensian Crusade went on for many years. In every city, hundreds and, in some cases, thousands of people were maimed, dispossessed, slaughtered by the King's soldiers, or burned at the stake by the officials of the Catholic Church. The most conservative estimate is that a quarter of a million people were slain. When the King's soldiers asked the Abbot of Citeaux how they should know the Catholics from the Cathars, the Abbot replied, "Kill them all, God will know his own.

The last Cathar stronghold was at Montsegur. The remaining Perfecti (Parfait) of the Cathar movement gathered there with their supporters. Having taken religious vows against the shedding of blood, the Perfecti were unable to defend themselves against the armies of the King, but, throughout the crusade against them, thousands of people, some not even of their faith, villagers, noblemen and their knights rose to their defense. After a ten-month siege 200 Cathar Perfecti and 300 defending soldiers stood off ten thousand soldiers of the King of France, but eventually the king's soldiers found a way through the defenses of the fortress, and the defenders could protect the Cathars no longer. On March 16th of the year 1244, the remaining Cathars surrendered and filed out to their captors. They were herded onto a great pyre surrounded by fencing and soldiers, yet through the flames they exited the world and entered into that liberation beyond the limitations and cruelty of this world, where no more torment could touch them.

Just before the fall of Montsegur, when the crusaders were preparing to storm the bastions if those within did not surrender, under cover of night and hidden by a cloud-like mist that moved as they moved, four Cathar Perfecti climbed down from the castle on a rope and lowered themselves down the steep side of the mountain. They carried with them a mysterious treasure. Some say the Holy Grail, others a collection of sacred texts, while others a sacramental sword in a carved wooden box. The cloud hid them as they passed into the fastness of the Pyrenees mountains to safety.

What this legend signifies is that something of the Cathars escaped destruction. Something was saved. Something was liberated from the grasp of their enemies. Whether it is past-life memories, or simply an archetypal and spiritual connection with those who have drunk from the same well of the living waters in the past, I cannot say. But something was transmitted, a spiritual legacy."

-- Rev. Steven Marshall

http://www.gnosis.org/ecclesia/homily_Montsegur

Penny –

> *I believe I was there as* ***Amiel Aicart, one of the four Cathar Parfaits that escaped over the wall*** *with the treasure. I have been drawn time and time again back to the Languedoc and the fortress of Rennes le Chateau near Montsegur where I believe I helped secure the treasure in the labyrinth of caves beneath. They were subsequently moved by the Templars but that is another story.*
>
> *I know that the Gnostic beliefs and motivations of the Cathars closely resonate with my own though polished into something more relevant to the current age. Perhaps it is as Rev. Marshall says, a past-life memory, but it strikes a chord deep in my knowing. I have been there before and am picking up the thread to continue the pattern...*

Nancy - I "get" that Nancy was the **Mayor of Beziers**. Béziers was a Languedoc stronghold of Catharism, which the Catholic Church condemned as heretical and which Catholic forces exterminated in the Albigensian Crusade.

Béziers was the first place to be attacked. The crusaders reached the town on July 21, 1209. Béziers' Catholics were given an ultimatum to hand over the heretics or leave before the crusaders besieged the city and to "avoid sharing their fate and perishing with them." However, they refused and resisted with the Cathars. The town was sacked on July 22, 1209 and in the bloody massacre, no one was spared, not even Catholic priests and those who took refuge in the churches. One of the commanders of the crusade was the Papal Legate Arnaud-Amaury). When asked by a Crusader how to tell Catholics from Cathars once they had taken the city, the abbot supposedly replied, ("Kill them all, for the Lord knoweth them that are His.")

They spared no one, irrespective of rank, sex or age, and put to the sword almost 20,000 people. After this great slaughter the whole city was despoiled and burnt.

Nancy lives part-time in the Languedoc today and conducts tours of the area.

Kathleen – I "get" that Kathleen was **Hughes de LaMothe**, a Knight from Gascony or Quercy, defender of the Languedoc during the Albigensian Crusade against the Cathars. The Crusaders regarded themselves as being "on God's business" and referred to themselves as "pilgrims". Like all crusades it was a war, declared by the Pope, (Innocent III) backed by the Roman Church with promises of remission of sins and a guaranteed place in heaven.

Teresa - *Cathar life*

I lived at Montsegur with you, shared many meals and died during the siege.

Don I "get" that Don was **Raymond de Perella**, commander of the knights at Montsegur who negotiated the surrender.

Amara -I "get" that Amara was **Hugon**, a Cathar Parfait that went over the wall with me to secret the treasure away. Together we have revisited the Languedoc in this lifetime.

Michael – I "get" that Michael was also **Hugon**.

(Author note – Remember multiple beings can reincarnate carrying forward aspects of a lifetime not to be forgotten and longing to be expressed)

Bo I "get" that Bo was **Guilhabert de Castres**, Bishop of the Cathar Church, and one of the Cathar Parfaits in that lifetime that perished at Montsegur. He has been called back to the area in this lifetime as well.

Joy –

"We were together in the monastery before it was invaded and were all killed. We did a lot of praying at the end and accepted our fate with calm and peace, knowing we could be reunited with God."

Dave – I "get" that Dave was **Peter (Pierre), Archbishop of Narbonne**. The extermination of the Albigenses having ended the war so long prosecuted against these people, Peter used all his efforts to pacify his diocese. But observing the method practiced in his time, he seized, according to that custom, all the goods which had belonged to the heretics, made all the inhabitants of Narbonne take oath to massacre anyone who should dare in the future to separate himself from the Roman orthodoxy, and in order to watch over, discover, and point out all the dissenters, introduced in 1231 into the city of Narbonne the St. Dominican friars. But the Albigenses were conquered, not subdued. An occasion having offered in 1234, the inhabitants rose in insurrection, and drove out their archbishop. Vainly he excommunicated them.

In order to return to his metropolis, after about a year's exile, Peter was obliged to descend to conditions the insurgents imposed upon him, among others, that of expelling from their city the Brother Preachers, and under his eyes, for greater safety, they invaded the convent of these brothers and put them to flight. Peter dared not recall them. In 1243, the archbishop Peter made the siege of the chateau of Montsegur, and taking it from the heretics. This was the last exploit of this belligerent prelate.

Knights Templar (1194-1250 AD)

After the First Crusade captured Jerusalem in 1099, many Christian pilgrims traveled to visit the Holy Places and fell victims to crime. Around 1119, a monastic order for the protection of these pilgrims was created called the *Poor Knights of Christ and the Temple of Solomon* was established by the Roman Catholic Church.

Upon arriving in Jerusalem, they began excavations of Temple Mount (Solomon's Temple) and secretly excavated many treasures and documents including the Arc of the Covenant.

- The "Templars" were initially endorsed by the Catholic church and exempted from taxes.
- They became the bankers of Europe and founded a system similar to credit cards and traveler's checks.
- They and amassed vast wealth and properties.
- They funded many building projects across Europe such as Chartres and Rosslyn Cathedral filled with symbolism of the Gnostic traditions.
- The Templars became masters at encoding esoteric knowledge in the Gothic cathedrals.
- Because of their wealth and power King Phillip IV of France and Pope Clement V conspired to discredit them and confiscate their wealth.
- They were arrested on Friday the 13th.
- Their ships and treasure had disappeared.
- Many of the Templars were tortured into false confessions then burned in front of Paris' Notre Dame Cathedral
- Many secrets and relics were hidden and have not resurfaced.

Penny –

We all carried wounds and impediments including pain, grief, sadness as well as anger at the way we saw things happening. Many could not understand why He choose the path he did and didn't do things differently. Many Essenes felt Jesus had abandoned them. We were blinded by our love for the man and his message. Many choose to deny or curse God for allowing what we believed to be a travesty to take place because we did not see the bigger picture.

The collective amnesia and emotional blocks we carry from that lifetime are barriers to our healing and vibrational growth. We are working together to remove the emotional impingements in our cellular memory from that lifetime and replace it with the opposite energy. Vows of not allowing forgiveness of ourselves and others, feelings of lack of power, and abandonment are being renounced so that we can move forward once again in service together.

I believe many of us have come back as a soul group as protectors of the ancient wisdom. Perhaps in our lifetime the artifacts, keys, and codes will resurface if we demonstrate the integrity to apply them wisely. Until then, we are asked to hold that space and become worthy stewards of the Divine mysteries.

Teresa - *Templar*

"I lived there in Jerusalem for around 30 years and became friends with Arabs, and Muslim.

I admired their advanced ethics and culture of the time. I died there of Cholera, or some kind of fever.

I trained as a soldier with you in Europe. After our training as Templars, and expending time in Jerusalem, we parted again."

Kevin – I "get" that Kevin was one of the Templar Knights who went to the Holy Land and brought back the treasure.

Kathleen – I "get" that Kathleen was **Jacques de Molay**, the 23rd and last Grand Master of the Knights Templar, leading the Order from 20 April 1292 until it was dissolved by order of Pope Clement V in 1307. Jacques de Molay's goal as Grand Master was to reform the Order and adjust it to the situation in the Holy Land during the waning days of the Crusades. As European support for the Crusades had dwindled, other forces were at work which sought to disband the Order and claim the wealth of the Templars as their own. King Philip IV of France, deeply in debt to the Templars, had Molay and many other French Templars arrested in 1307 and tortured into making false confessions. When Molay later retracted his confession, Philip had him burned upon a scaffold on an island in the River Sein in front of Notre Dame de Paris in March 1314.

Nancy – I "get" that Nancy was also **Jacques de Molay**. Today Nancy is a Knight's Templar in France.

"Yes, I was a "grid carrier", one who held the energy

for the planet, the people, the great heart. I

remember and have stepped into this unfinished

Templar intention once again, hoping to call into

alignment the One Universe.

Yes, we had secrets and practiced ancient wisdom

unknown to many, but finally, we will help people

re-unite again. It's time to step forward and

remember your place in the world order. Get ready."

Barbara –

"During the Knights Templar times. This was when there was a group of 12 of us that guarded the artifacts of Solomon's Temple. Penny's role was to write about each of the artifacts. What is was, it's purpose but not how to use is. We were told by Spirit that the KT would probably come to take the artifacts, so we were to catalog all the items. Penny was the head of our group, so she organized and managed the process. Each of us knew how to work with the artifacts yet the KT did not know this. In fact, no one outside of our group knew we had been secretly working with the artifacts to fully understand how to use each one.

The raids on the temple occurred over a span of time. At one point they started interrogating our group to find out about the artifacts. They were threatening torture and death. Penny thought it best, and our group agreed, to give them the artifact catalog, thinking that would pacify the KT and they'd leave us alone. We quickly made a copy of the catalog before giving them the original. Unfortunately, this did not pacify them, it inflamed the situation. The artifact catalog convinced them we knew how to use the artifacts. They wanted it for power and control.

Penny convinced the group to let her be the sacrificial lamb. She and only she would admit to knowing how to use the artifacts since she was the leader of our group. She would say that wisdom and knowledge was pass down only to her. The rest of us were interrogated and supported her story. Little did we know she decided to refuse to provide them the "how to" information. She was tortured and then killed. They murdered her in front of us. I can feel in my body it was gut wrenching and horrible to watch. It broke my heart.

How does this reflect in this life? I've always liked Penny, felt comfortable and safe around her as well as felt respect toward her, even when I barely knew her. I cannot bring myself to remember her murder. I sense it would bring up a tremendous amount of anguish that's not ready to be remembered or felt at this time."

Jami -

"I was afraid and panic the first time I saw a Templar Knights uniform. To this day, I can't watch battle scenes from movies from this time period. I realize this was a lifetime for me of great sadness, confusion, and betrayal.

I have had many life times with in the crusades. Then I sense I had a lifetime believing I could help Rome protect the pilgrims but came to see and understand Rome's true agenda and felt betrayed. I then switched sides and fought from within the order to hide what we were finding until it could be safe for humanity., the inquisition and so forth—from aggressor to innocent farm girl, from a "keeper of the mystery" and the sacred ways to one who represented Rome to stop the truth. The time of the Templar Knights brought more confusion, quest, promise of advancement and guarantees of Heaven if you fought for this cause. I think I joined this cause to serve Rome and protect the pilgrims and then saw Rome's agenda and felt betrayed. I then switched sides and fought from within the order to hide what we were finding until it could be safe for humanity.

I believe my ultimate role at this time was to be a part of a special team that helped facilitate where the Templar's hidden treasures would be relocated to for safe keeping until the time was destined to come forward. Recently I was watching a TV show with Penny "The lost treasures of Oak Island," and I felt myself mesmerized. The other night when I was investigating You Tube history about the Templar Knights, I came across a Forbidden History segment that invoked a remembrance in my being that we took Templar treasures that carry Truth for humanity about our true history to Scotland and to Oak Island in Nova Scotia. Perhaps they have been moved since as it feels right in my soul that sacred treasures move locations throughout time with the "keepers" that are charged for their safety.

I see for myself that many of my soul group were in these timelines again trying to protect and serve our people that knew deeper wisdom. It seems that we tend to incarnate together during "revolutionary" times and times of great historical significance. So much of these timelines from the Cathars to the Templars is blurry for me. I feel deep pain and confusion still within me from the atrocities. We had to do and endure awful things just to survive, no matter which side we were sharing loyalties, and even that got confusing."

Margaret –

"The most I could get about this lifetime is that *I was born and grew up in a Knight's Templar in Portugal. My parents were Knight's Templars. A few years ago, I visited this castle once in this life which is near Fatima."*

Joy –

We were Knights and worked at Solomon's temple together retrieving artifacts and burying high-ranking people who had passed. We escaped together and went to England and then America.

Don – I "get" that Don was one of the Templar Knights rounded up and burned on Friday 13th.

Will - I "get" that Will was one of the Templar knights who went to the Holy land and brought back the treasure.

Dave – I "get" that Dave was one of the Templar Knights who went to the holy land and brought back the treasure

Bo - I "get" that once again, Bo was a warrior for the church and one of the Templar knights rounded up and burned on Friday 13th.

Michael – I "get" that Michael was one of the Knights Templar that helped bring the treasure to the new world.

Chartres

Chartres Cathedral, also known as **Cathedral of Our Lady of Chartres**, is a medieval Catholic cathedral of the Latin Church located in Chartres, France, about 80 kilometers (50 mi) southwest of Paris. It is considered one of the finest examples of French Gothic architecture and is a UNESCO World Heritage Site.

Constructed in 30 years without a plan or blueprint by master builders employed by the Templars. It codifies in stone both esoteric and biblical wisdom.

I was one of the Templars that helped build Chartres. I have been drawn to this place ever since I first saw it and have visited several times.

Here I am in 2011 walking the labyrinth.

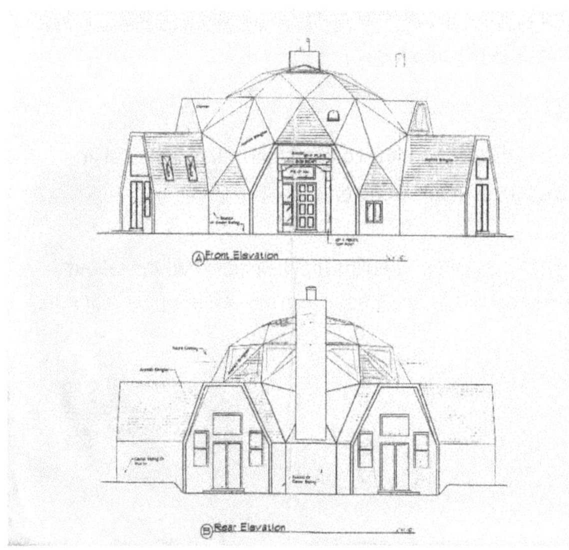

I have been a designer for over 35 years and had my own design firm. I have designed and built structures based on sacred geometry including labyrinths, mandala gardens and a geodesic adobe home in New Mexico.

Teresa - *Notre Dame-Paris, France Europe*

"I was a Builder Mason (Of the Masonic Order) Today this will be classified as Construction. He...heh...

I also had a bitter memory of this, in this life time. I was yelled and punished for saying that a Church looked somehow like Notre Dame. I was told that I did not knew what I was talking about, and to stop repeating like a parrot. That shut me up and made me not want to mention any thing to any adult. It caused me to doubt myself until today.

As a group of Masonic Builders, we were assigned to build Cathedrals in different locations of France, Sacred areas, vortexes to Higher Dimensions they were also in alignment with Constellations to increased Energy of the areas.

Alas, we died almost at the same time as word got out what the real purpose of the Cathedrals was, and we were executed in front of the Notre Dame as Heretics for calling ourselves Great Architects. Blasphemy.

In this lifetime that explains why I loved the designs of my father who was a Civil Engineer for multiple buildings. The designs were carried to the final completions of the buildings and construction by him during his positions as Mayor of the city where I was born."

(Author's Note – Guilds were assembled of craftsmen for construction of the cathedrals, thus the origins of the Masonic orders that survive unto today.)

Amara – I "get" that Amara was also involved with the construction of the cathedral at Chartres. Together we have visited Chartres in this lifetime.

Loras – I "get" that Loras was one of the Knight's Templars that helped imbed the sacred geometry in the cathedral of Chartres. In this lifetime Loras constructs large copper sculptures based on sacred geometry patterns.

Acoma (1340-1392 AD)

I was on my way to an appointment in Santa Fe, New Mexico. On a divided highway, I had moved into the left turn lane, perpendicular to traffic as I tried to find a street sign to confirm I was going the right way. The next thing I knew my air bag went off. I had no idea what had hit me. I pulled off to the side of the road out of the traffic and got out with my cell phone. There was a motorcycle imbedded in my front bumper and there, at the base of a light post, was a man who must have been catapulted into it head first without a helmet.

I called 911 and began to tell the operator why I could not give the man CPR because he was obviously dead. A man/angel put his arms around my shoulders and led me away saying that I did not have to see this anymore. When the police arrived, the man/angel disappeared.

I was unhurt and as I sat in the police car while they investigated the crash and I tried to make sense of things. I searched for meaning in something that seemed so senseless. Eventually I consulted two psychics who confirmed that this was indeed a karmic situation. The man had been my husband in a previous lifetime and had beaten me to death in a jealous rage. We contacted him on the other side and he was overjoyed that finally he had been released from this karmic burden. He said that I would not suffer any legal repercussions from the accident and I did not.

I was given another piece of this sometime later. We could not find my son and it had been several days since anyone had seen him. We contacted a remote viewer and he led us to a spot on the Acoma reservation that we homed in on Google Earth. Instead of this being where my son was, it was where my husband had killed me in that previous lifetime. My son now was my sister then and witnessed the event. Evidently the energy surrounding this incidence was so strong there was a bleed-through from other dimensions and the psychic was picking up on my previous lifetime. My son checked in and he was fine.

Teresa - *Acoma Native*

"Here in the United States I was born 3 times as a Native.
One in Florida, where I had a tranquil happy life as a woman but died young.
Another was in the Dakotas where I was a Sioux warrior.
The third was at Acoma, New Mexico, where my job was hunting for the welfare of the tribe. I lived for 18 years past my 18th birthday and died by accident while hunting.

In that life time at Acoma we were related. You were my younger sister. We interacted very much as children. I saw us playing with mud and sticks, building houses.... always playing building.

I have met in this lifetime many Native Americans from New Mexico, who recognize me as one of their own.

I was told I was not born in this country, but my Karma is here in the U.S.A."

Janice - *Your Acoma lifetime:*

"Yes, I have been drawn to Acoma this lifetime and have gone there many times. I was an artisan who made pots (also did this in France) and also created dance clothing. The dance clothing, I made was embellished with small crystals that hung from leather straps that would "sing" when the dancers turned. They would also sparkle in the sunlight. The mica pieces were also used, and they reflected the gold rays.

I was always immediately drawn to the painting you did of the three Natives with colorful robes. Every time I came to your home, I could not help but be mesmerized by it."

Harry – Harry and I went on a vacation to New Mexico and visited the Acoma pueblo. He had a negative reaction to the experience and couldn't wait to get out of New Mexico. It seems he was my son in that lifetime and witnessed my husband beating me to death.

Joan of Arc (1412-1431 AD)

Jeanne d'Arc was born into a peasant family at Domremy in north-east France. Joan said she received visions of the Archangel Michael, Saint Margaret and Saint Catherine instructing her to support Charles VII and recover France from English domination late in the Hundred Years' War. The uncrowned King Charles VII sent Joan to the siege of Orleans. She gained prominence after the siege was lifted only nine days later. Several additional swift victories led to Charles VII's coronation at Reims. This long-awaited event boosted French morale and paved the way for the final French victory.

On 23 May 1430 she was captured at Compiegne by the Burgundian faction which was allied with the English. She was later handed over to the English and then put on trial by the pro-English Bishop of Beauvais Pierre Cauchon on a variety of charges. After Cauchon declared her guilty she was burned at the stake on 30 May 1431, dying at about nineteen years of age.

When Joan refused to submit to rape by her captors, the Bishop pronounced her an ungrateful sorcerer.

Twenty-five years after her execution, an inquisitional court authorized by Pope Callixtus III examined the trial, debunked the charges against her, pronounced her innocent, and declared her a martyr. In the 16th century she became a symbol of the Catholic League, and in 1803 she was declared a national symbol of France by Napoleon Bonaparte. She was beatified in 1909 and canonized in 1920.

Penny -

I am fortunate to live at a time and, at least within the confines of Sedona, in a place where my "voices" are valued for their wisdom rather than feared for their truth. Once again, I must step forward and speak my truth. "I am not afraid. I was born to do this" said Joan of Arc.

Joan carried a banner the words "Jesus Mary "(Magdalene) written on it.

Many of those that were part of the soul group at that time in history have presented themselves in my life today. Many of the generals I commanded in that lifetime have shown up as heroes in my life this time around to assist me in my journey - from helping me run a business, form a foundation, or help me move my furniture to a new state. We continue to show up for each other without question because we have fought together in battles of life before. Childhood friends then return as companions in later life. A judge then who recognized subterfuge then but was threatened into silence then is fearful and has trouble stepping up in integrity today. Another who championed my exoneration then champions equally maligned causes today.

*Interestingly, I "get" that my prosecutor at that time, **Bishop Cauchon**, has returned as former **Pope Benedict** who was Cardinal Ratzinger, head of the present-day Inquisition, The Sacred Congregation of the Holy Office.*

Don - I "get" that Don was **Constable Richemont** who was head of the reconciliation between Burgundy and France. He was instrumental in clearing Joan's name and reputation.

Will - I "get" that Will was **Pothon de Saintrailles,** one of Joan's generals.

Janice -

"As for Joan of Arc, I was the male guardian who rode beside her into the battles. Again, another warrior lifetime. We had a common commitment and goal."

I "got" several months ago that Janice was **Sire Bertrand de Poulengy**, a knight who was in service to Joan.

"Aha: Thanks so much for the "jog" of the memory...I got overwhelming goosebumps, crown chakra going off when I read the name Sir Bertrand de Poulengy! I recognized the name immediately. Ashtar had given it to me."

Bo - I "get" that Bo was **Sire Jean de Novelpont de Metz,** a Knight in the service of Joan.

Kevin - I "get" that Kevin was a soldier under Joan's command.

Amara - I "get" that Amara was **Raoul de Gancourt**, Grand Master of the Palace.

Nancy - I "get" that Nancy was **Charles VII** of Valois, Dauphine of France who was manipulated by the church.

Vicky - I "get" that Vicky was **Queen Yolanda of Aragon**, Rene de Anjou's mother, the Dauphine's mother-in-law, who championed Joan.

Gordon - I "get" that Gordon was **Etienne de Vignolles ("LaHire")**, a close comrade of Joan of Arc. He was one of the few military leaders who believed in her and the inspiration she brought, and he fought alongside her at Orleans.

Jim I "get" that Jim was **John of Orleans, Count of Dunois ("the Bastard of Orleans**) managed to successfully force the siege to be lifted and won battle of Orleans.

Jami **–** I "get" that Jami was Joan's brother, **Pierre d'Arc.**

> *"I had heard that I was a brother to Joan of Arc and fought alongside her. In this lifetime, I still look to her for leadership and feel watchful over that she is happy and has her needs met. To this day, I experience her as a leader in a paradigm shift and am relieved to see her in a gentle time of her life as a well-loved and supported wisdom keeper and community leadership that many of our soul group look to for intuitive and level-headed guidance and reassurance."*

Harry – I "get" that Harry was one of the judges called in to condemn Joan in her prison cell. When he tried to object that the evidence obviously was fabricated, he was threatened with death and therefore remained silent. In this lifetime truth is of the utmost importance in his life and he supports and defends me on many levels.

Kathleen - I "get" that Kathleen was **Talbot,** one of the British generals defeated by Joan at Orleans.

Dave - I "get" that Dave was **Richard Guetin**, Talbot's lieutenant, that Joan defeated at Orleans.

Channeling from Joan of Arc through Penny Genter

My dearest Penny,

Looking back at the time in which I lived, it is hard to realize the importance of the mission I was sent on. The feeling in all of France was one of defeat at the hands of the British. I was sent to turn the tide of history and to restore the rightful descendants of the bloodline to the throne. While the immediate effect was not felt while I was alive, it indeed stemmed an assault that was felt long after my sojourn on earth.

The fact that I was a mere maid, uneducated, and "clueless" of military knowledge was a clear sign that this was no ordinary mission but one that had the fingerprints of God all over it. I merely stepped forward and assumed the armor I was promised. Much has been made about the way I commanded the forces and how I stood my own in the face of the most learned and treacherous men of the time, but I merely allowed the voices of reason to speak through me. I was merely the vessel of divine leadership.

I grew weary of the constant treachery, but it was something I had agreed to do, and promised God I would. As Mother Mary has told you: "We are held in the hands of God". My "voices" were strong as are yours. The time I lived in was not receptive to them as is yours today. As you say – timing is everything in life.

I was ready to exit that brief lifetime and suffered little when the flames came to take my earthly body. The later canonization was meant as an apology for the dastardly subterfuge inflicted upon my poor life. It matters not. My wish is that those who study my life will remember my words – "I am not afraid. I was born to do this" – and so I was. Amen.

Jeanne d'Arc

Lucrezia Tornabouni (1427-1482AD)

(slight overlap with the Joan of Arc lifetime with aspects incarnated at the same time)

Lucrezia Tornabouni was a writer and influential political adviser. Connected by birth to two of the most powerful families in the 15th-century Italy, she later married Piero di Cosimo de' Medici, connecting herself to another of the most powerful families in Italy and extending her own power and influence. She had significant political influence during the rule of her husband and then her son, Lorenzo (the Magnificent), the "Father of the Renaissance". She worked to support the needs of the poor and religious in the region, supporting several institutions. She was a patron of the arts and also wrote poems and plays herself.

Lucrezia and Piero made sure that their children acquired good taste in literary culture and the fine arts and also hired tutors to educate them in such subjects as philosophy, business and accounting, and politics. Lorenzo's mother was a writer of sonnets and a friend to poets and philosophers of the Medici Academy. She became her son's advisor after the deaths of his father and uncle. She influenced her family's appreciation of the arts and was a strong impetus for the flourishing of the Renaissance.

Penny –

In this lifetime I am most at home in the world of art and literature. According to Sophia's Mirror – The Treasure Map to Your Soul Incarnation, my Field of Destiny is" Making the World More Beautiful". Everything I do is with that intention. I live in one of the most beautiful places on earth where art is expressed and appreciated. It is where I feel most comfortable. I was more than enraptured at a recent movie about Florence and the Uffizi Gallery. I felt as if I had come home – perhaps I had...

In Kathleen McGowan's book, ***The Poet Prince****, she details much of the period around Lorenzo de Medici and the birth of the Renaissance. It was like reading my family history.*

Elizabeth - I "get" that Elizabeth was **Piero**, the son of Cosimo de' Medici the Elder and Contessina de' Bardi and my husband in that lifetime. During his father's life he did not play an extensive role due to his perpetual poor health, the source of his nickname. His brother Giovanni was named as Cosimo's executor but predeceased his father. In 1461, Piero was the last Medici elected to the office of Gonfaloniere. His gout often kept him confined to bed. This meant that his bedroom effectively became his office where he would conduct political meetings and led to the Medici palace becoming the seat of government.

He continued the family's tradition of artistic patronage, He also continued to collect rare books, adding many to the Medici collections. All his family is probably portrayed in the famous painting by Botticelli, called "Madonna del Magnificat" (Madonna of the Magnificat), where Lucrezia Tornabouni appears as the Virgin Mary

In this lifetime Elizabeth was an accomplished poet and Shakespearean scholar and teacher. She also had a previous lifetime as the composer Richard Wagner.

Amara I "get" that in that lifetime Amara was **Giuliano de' Medici** who) was the second son of Piero de' Medici (the Gouty) and Lucrezia Tornabouni. As co-ruler of Florence, with his brother Lorenzo the Magnificent, he complemented his brother's image as the "patron of the arts" with his own image as the handsome, sporting, "golden boy." As the opening stroke of the Piazzi Conspiracy, he was assassinated on Sunday, 26 April 1478 in the Duomo of Florence, Santa Maria del Fiore, by Francesco de 'Piazzi and Bernardo Baroncelli. He was killed by a sword wound to the head and was stabbed 23 times.

Lorenzo adopted Giulio di Giuliano de' Medici, Giuliano's illegitimate son by his mistress Fioretta Gorini, who went on to become Pope Clement VI who refused to annul King Henry VIII marriage to Catherine in order for him to marry Anne Boleyn. The Pope responded to the marriage by excommunicating Henry from the Catholic Church. Ultimately Henry led the English Parliament to pass the Act of Supremacy (1534) that established the independent Church of England and breaking from the Catholic Church.

Jim - I "get" that in that lifetime Jim was **Lorenzo de' Medici** (1449 – 1492) who was an Italian statesman and *de facto* ruler of the Florentine Republic He was one of the most powerful and enthusiastic patrons of the Renaissance. Also known as **Lorenzo the Magnificent** by contemporary Florentines, he was a magnate, diplomat, politician and patron of scholars, artists and poets. He is well known for his contribution to the art world by sponsoring artists such as Botticelli and Michelangelo. His life coincided with the mature phase of Italian Renaissance and his death coincided with the end of the Golden Age of Florence. The fragile peace that he helped maintain among the various Italian states collapsed with his death.

Lorenzo's grandfather, Cosimo de' Medici, was the first member of the Medici family to combine running the Medici Bank with leading the Republic of Florence. Cosimo was one of the wealthiest men in Europe and spent a very large portion of his fortune in government and philanthropy. He was a patron of the arts and funded public works.

Lorenzo, considered the brightest of the five children of Piero and Lucrezia, was tutored by a diplomat and bishop, a humanist philosopher, and a Greek scholar. Piero sent Lorenzo on many important diplomatic missions when he was still a youth, which included trips to Rome to meet the pope and other important religious and political figures.

Lorenzo was groomed for power and assumed a leading role in the state upon the death of his father in 1469, when he was twenty. Already drained by his grandfather's building projects and constantly stressed by mismanagement, wars, and political expenses, the bank's assets contracted seriously during the course of Lorenzo's lifetime.

In the aftermath of the Piazzi Conspiracy and the punishment of Pope Sixtus IV's supporters, the Medici and Florence suffered from the wrath of the Holy See, which seized all the Medici assets Sixtus could find, excommunicated Lorenzo and the entire government of Florence and ultimately put the entire Florentine city-state under interdict. When these moves had little effect, Sixtus formed a military alliance with King Ferdinand I of Naples, whose son, led an invasion of the Florentine Republic, still ruled by Lorenzo. Lorenzo rallied the citizens and ultimately resolved the crisis. That success enabled Lorenzo to secure constitutional changes within the Florentine Republic's government, which further enhanced his own power.

Lorenzo's court included artists such as Piero and Antonio del Pollaiuolo, Andrea del Verrocchio, Leonardo da Vinci, Sandro Botticelli, Domenico Ghirlandaio and Michelangelo Buonarroti, who were masters in the 15th-century Renaissance. Although he did not commission many works himself, he helped them secure commissions from other patrons. Lorenzo was an artist himself, writing poetry in his native Tuscan.

His grandfather, Cosimo had started the collection of books that became the Medici Library and Lorenzo expanded it. Lorenzo's agents retrieved from the East large numbers of classical works, and he employed a large workshop to copy his books and disseminate their content across

Europe. He supported the development of humanism through his circle of scholarly friends. They studied Greek philosophers and attempted to merge the ideas of Plato with Christianity.

Toward the end of Lorenzo's life, Florence came under the spell of Dominican priest Girolamo Savonarola, who he had invited to Florence. Savonarola believed Christians had strayed too far into Greco-Roman culture. Called the "Bonfire of the Vanities", his supporters collected and publicly burned thousands of objects such as cosmetics, art, and books in Florence, Italy.

Lorenzo died unexpectedly at age 43 on 9 April 1492 after a visit from Savonarola.

Lorenzo's heir was his eldest son, Piero di Lorenzo de' Medici, known as "Piero the Unfortunate". He squandered his father's patrimony and brought down the Medici dynasty in Florence. The second son, Giovanni, who became Pope Leo X soon afterwards, restored it, but it was not made wholly secure again until the accession of his great-grandson from a branch line of the family, Cosimo I de' Medici (Penny).

Kathleen – I "get" that Kathleen was **Lucretia Donati** (Colombina), soul-mate and mistress of Lorenzo de Medici. Forced into a political dynastic marriage, Lorenzo continued his heart alliance with Lucretia. Beautifully detailed in Kathleen McGowan's book *the Poet Prince*.

Michael – I "get" that Michael was **Magdalena**, beloved daughter of Lorenzo de' Medici and Clarise Orsini.

In this lifetime Michael is drawn to Raphael's images of cherubs and angels and collects artwork of the period.

Cosimo I de' Medici (1519-1574AD)

Cosimo I de' Medici, Grand Duke of Tuscany was born in Florence. He came into power at 17 when the Duke, Alessandro de' Medici, was assassinated without leaving a legitimate heir. Cosimo was from a different branch of the family however many of the influential men in the city favored him. Cosimo proved strong-willed, astute and ambitious.

Cosimo obtained recognition from Charles V as head of the Florentine state which allowed him to free Tuscany from the Imperial garrisons and to increase as much as possible its independence from the overwhelming Spanish influence in Italy. He laid siege to Sienna and annexed it to his territories. In 1569, Pope Pius V elevated him to the rank of Grand Duke of Tuscany. In the last ten years of his rein to his son and successor Francesco I de' Medici.

Cosimo was a lavish patron of the arts. He is best known today for the creation of the Uffizi ("offices"). Originally intended as a means of consolidating his administrative committees, agencies, and guilds, it now houses one of the world's most important collections of art, much of it commissioned and/or owned by various Medici. He was an important patron of the arts.

His gardens at Villa di Castello, were designed to announce a new golden age for Florence and to express the magnificence and virtues of the Medici. They were decorated with fountains, a labyrinth, a grotto and ingenious "water jokes," and were a prototype of the Italian Renaissance garden. They had a profound influence on later Italian and French gardens through the eighteenth century. Cosimo was also an enthusiast of alchemy.

Penny –

I must feel Cosimo's reverence for beauty, expressed in art and gardens. This has been a passion of the last 40 years of my life. I was recently "blown away" by the new film, Florence and the Uffizi Gallery, and felt an important connection to the place and the time. I have reread Kathleen McGowan's book, ***The Poet Prince****, three times reveling in her descriptions of the art in the Uffizi. Though I have yet to experience this in person, I am sure it will soon be on my travel agenda as I feel it calling me home...*

Victoria – I "get that Victoria was Maria Salviati, Cosimo's mother.

Jim - I "get" that Jim was Cosimo's wife, **Eleonora di Toledo** (1522 – 1562), the daughter the Spanish viceroy of Naples. Her face is still familiar to many because of her solemn and distant portraits by Agnolo Bronzino. The most famous of them, with her son Giovanni, hangs in the Uffizi Gallery. She provided the Medici with the Pitti Palace and seven sons to ensure male succession and four daughters to connect the Medici with noble and ruling houses in Italy. She was a patron of the new Jesuit order, and her private chapel in the Palazzo Vecchio was decorated by Bronzino, who had originally arrived in Florence to provide festive decor for her wedding. She died, with her sons Giovanni and Garzia, in 1562, when she was only forty; all three of them were struck down by malaria while traveling to Pisa.

Amara - I "get" that Amara was **Giovanni di Cosimo I de' Medici** (29 September 1544 – 20 November 1562), also known as Giovanni de' Medici the Younger, was an Italian cardinal.

He was born in Florence, the second son of Cosimo I de' Medici, Grand Duke of Tuscany, and Eleonora of Toledo. While his elder brother Francesco went on to a political and military career, Giovanni had reserved for him the ecclesiastical career.

After having been Archbishop of Pisa, he was created cardinal in Santa Maria in Domenica by Pope Pius IV in the consistory of 31 January 1560, aged only seventeen.

Probably already suffering from tuberculosis, Giovanni died two years later in Livorno, from a malaria attack. His mother and his brother Garzia died of the latter illness a few days later.

Kathleen – I "get" that Kathleen was **Agnolo Bronzino**, a Florentine Mannerist painter. He lived all his life in Florence, and from his late 30s was kept busy as the court painter of Cosimo I de' Medici, Grand Duke of Tuscany. He was mainly a portraitist but also painted many religious subjects, and a few allegorical subjects. Many portraits of the Medicis exist in several versions with varying degrees of participation by Bronzino himself, as Cosimo was a pioneer of the copied portrait sent as a diplomatic gift

Vicky – I "get" that Vicky was my son and heir **Francesco I** (25 March 1541 – 19 October 1587), the second Grand Duke of Tuscany,

In this lifetime Vicky has lived in Florence.

Anne Boleyn (1511-1536 AD)

Ann Boleyn was Queen of England from 1533 to 1536 as the second wife of King Henry VIII. Henry's marriage to Anne, and her subsequent execution by beheading, made her a key figure in the political and religious upheaval that was the start of the English Reformation.

Ann was educated in the Netherlands and France, largely as a maid of honor to Claude of France. She returned to England in 1522 to marry her cousin James Butler but the marriage plans were broken up by Cardinal Wolseley and instead she secured a post at court as maid of honor to Henry VIII's wife, Catherine of Aragon.

In 1523 Anne was secretly betrothed to Henry Percy but Cardinal Wolsey broke the betrothal and Anne was sent back home to Hever castle. In early 1926 Henry began his pursuit of Anne. She resisted his attempts to seduce her, refusing to become his mistress as her sister Mary had been. It soon became the one absorbing object of Henry's desires to annul his marriage to Queen Catherine, so he would be free to marry Anne. When it became clear that Pope Clemett VII would not annul the marriage, the breaking of the power of the Catholic Church in England began.

Henry and Anne married on 25 January 1533, after a secret marriage November 14, 1532. On 25 May 1533 Thomas Cramer declared Henry and Catherine's marriage null and void. Five days later he declared Henry and Anne's marriage valid. Shortly afterwards, the Pope decreed sentences of excommunication against Henry and Cramer. As a result of this marriage and those excommunications, the break between the Church of England was brought under the King's control. Anne was crowned Queen of England on 1 June 1533. On 7 September she gave birth to the future Queen Elizabeth I. Henry was disappointed to have a daughter rather than a son but hoped a son would follow and professed to love Elizabeth. Anne subsequently had three miscarriages and by March 1536 Henry was courting Jane Seymour.

Henry had Anne investigated for high treason in April 1536. On 2 May she was arrested and sent to the Tower of London, where she was tried before a jury of peers – which included Henry Percy, her former betrothed, and her own uncle, Thomas Howard. She was found guilty on 15 May. She was beheaded four days later. Modern historians view the charges against her, which included, adultery, incest, and plotting to kill the king as unconvincing.

Penny –

I was raised in the Church of England, the legacy of Anne Boleyn. My middle name is Anne. In high school I performed the soliloquy of Anne Boleyn from the play ***Anne of the Thousand Days*** *as my senior dissertation. As long as I can remember I have felt an attachment to Anne Boleyn. Walking through the Tower of London, and Hampton Court I did not feel apprehension, but familiarity before I ever knew what that was about. Anne unwittingly began the breaking down of the tethers that hold many of the faithful enslaved to the Catholic church. It was a beginning...*

Teresa

"We were almost the same age. I was born to a street girl, of unknown father. I was sold at a very young age as a prop to a woman to help her beg. Later at 12 or 13 I landed in the hands of a man who used girls for prostitution, and robbery at night. He beat us if we did not bring in enough money.

So, I run away with another girl who became my best friend then, and also in this life time. She was a great friend. (Thanks, Frederika). During the winter I got sick and died with Pneumonia. She followed very close.

We were very close to the Tower of London. I learned about you, and your life thru the gossip of the rabble in the streets. I envied your position and that you had food.

Being an empathic person, I could feel your distress, I mourned for you, when we were told that the Queen had been beheaded.

Extra information: Group souls when incarnated feel for each other, especially if you are in the proximity of each other. I asked not to be born ever in England again."

Jami **–** I "get" that Jami was **Mary Boleyn**, Anne's sister whose family enjoyed considerable influence during the reign of King Henry VIII. She was one of his mistresses from a period of roughly 1521 to 1526. It has been rumored that she bore two of the king's children.

"I am told I was Anne's sister, Mary. In watching a movie recently—The other Boleyn Girl-- I felt myself transported in time to where once again I was in living as a female in an out-of-balance masculine run world, indeed as Mary Boleyn. Although all the children in the family were "played" and manipulated by their father and uncle, in doing what was expected of us for family advancement, I feel this was a life time that for the most part I did my best to bring love and honor to situations that may not otherwise have had that experience. I believe this was a lifetime to not make wrong the order that what was, but to find ways to speak my truth and live in grace true to my ethics as best I could, within the society structure at the time.

I also believe this life time marked my exhaustion with being a female at the expense and manipulation of male lust and power, and I entered a period of lifetimes in which I felt the way to be safest on this planet was to start incarnating into the Catholic institution as a nun. The only way I saw to reconnect to the sacred feminine on this plant. If you can't beat them, join them and try to make changes from the inside. I went on to have many lifetimes within the Catholic church, trying to maintain and connect to what was sacred, striving to remember and connect with what was Truth within the lie.

It is interesting to note, that in my current lifetime, most of the significant people in my life, especially all four of my housemates, and my best friend were all incarnated in the key roles of Anne Boleyn's lifetime. We all now treat each other with respect and honor.

Joel – I "get" that Joel was Mary's first husband, **William Carey,** who was a courtier and favorite of King Henry VIII of England. He served the king as a Gentleman of the Privy chamber, and Esquire of the Body to the King. Shortly after their marriage, Mary became the mistress of King Henry VIII. The Boleyns received grants of land, and Carey himself profited from his wife's unfaithfulness, being granted manors and estates by the King while it was in progress. William Carey did not live to enjoy his sister-in-law's prosperity, since he died of the sweating sickness (hantavirus) the following year. He died greatly in debt, and his wife was reduced to pawning her jewelry before Anne Boleyn arranged a pension for her.

"Recently, I was introduced to a movie, set in a time frame that does intrigue me very much, even to this day. As the movie unfolded, I found myself ready to yell judgmental remarks toward a certain character in the film, which was a very curious sensation. It's unlike me to get so caught up and carried away like that toward a character in a movie! Here's the thing: I couldn't believe William Carey, would stand by and allow his wife to become a mistress to King Henry VIII, regardless of any situation. How could a man simply stand by and allow such a thing? According to what Penny gets, I was that man! (Wimp) and Jami was my wife who I allowed to be taken by the king! Talk about selling your soul and giving away true wealth, in exchange for what - earthly possessions and position...wow! One could say; that's just the way things were done in those times and there was really no choice but to allow the king to have his way. Maybe this is why this struck me so. I believe that we always have a choice and that we can rise above the status quo and stand our ground even at the threat of death. At least we will have remained true to ourselves and not sell out. Maybe this is why in this life I had the chance to either give in or stand my moral ground. I passed the test and stood tall for what I truly believe in regardless of the consequences. I have been shown that we are always doing the best we can and if we could do better, we would do better. No judgment, only understanding.
So, William (Joel), it's amazing to me that you allowed yourself to take the road you traveled. Yet, you're off the hook."

Kevin– I "get" that Kevin was Mary's second husband, **William Stafford**, a soldier from a good family but with few prospects. This secret marriage to a man considered beneath her station angered both Henry VIII and her sister, Queen Anne, and resulted in Mary's banishment from the royal court. She spent the remainder of her life in obscurity, dying seven years after Anne's execution.

Paul I "get" that Paul was **George Boleyn,** 2nd Viscount was an English courtier and nobleman, and the brother of queen consort Anne Boleyn. This made him the brother-in-law of King Henry VIII and the maternal uncle of Queen Elizabeth I of England. A prominent figure in the politics of the early 1530s, he was wrongly convicted of incest with Anne during the period of her trial for high treason. They were both executed as a result.

Bo – I "get" that in that lifetime Bo was Anne's Uncle **Thomas Howard**, 3rd Duke of Norfolk. Howard was an able soldier and was often employed in military operations was a prominent Tudor politician. He was an uncle of two of the wives of Henry VIII: Anne Boleyn and Catherine Howard and played a major role in the machinations behind these marriages. After falling from favor in 1546, he was stripped of the dukedom and imprisoned in the Tower, avoiding execution when the King died. He was released on the accession of Queen Mary I. He aided Mary in securing her throne, setting the stage for alienation between his Catholic family and the Protestant royal line that would be continued by Queen Elizabeth I.

Dave - I "get" that Dave was **Henry VIII**, King of England and the first English King of Ireland and continued the nominal claim by English monarchs to the Kingdom of France. Henry was the second monarch of the Tudor dynasty, succeeding his father, Henry VII.

Besides his six marriages, Henry VIII is known for his role in the separation of the Church of England from the Roman Catholic Church. His disagreements with the Pope led to his separation of the Church of England from papal authority, with himself, as king, as the Supreme Head of the Church of England and to the Dissolution of the Monasteries. Because his principal dispute was with papal authority, rather than with doctrinal matters, he remained a believer in core Catholic theological teachings despite his excommunication from the Roman Catholic Church. Henry oversaw the legal union of England and Wales. He is also well known for a long personal rivalry with both Francis I of France and the Holy Roman Emperor Charles V, with whom he frequently warred.

Domestically, Henry is known for his radical changes to the English Constitution, ushering in the theory of the divine right of kings to England. Besides asserting the sovereign's supremacy over the Church of England, thus initiating the English Reformation, he greatly expanded royal power. Charges of treason and heresy were commonly used to quash dissent, and those accused were often executed without a formal trial, by means of bills of attainer.

Kathleen – I "get" that Kathleen was **Elizabeth Boleyn**, Countess of Wiltshire who was an English noblewoman, noted for being the mother of Anne Boleyn and as such the maternal grandmother of Elizabeth 1 of England. The eldest daughter of Thomas Howard, 2nd Duke of Norfolk and his first wife. She married Thomas Boleyn sometime in the later 15th century.

John –

I "get" that John was **Thomas Boleyn, 1st Earl of Wiltshire, 1st Earl of Ormond, 1st Viscount Rochford** (c. 1477 – 12 March 1539) was an English diplomat and politician in the Tudor era. He was born at the family home, Hever Castle, Kent, which had been purchased by his grandfather Sir Geoffrey Boleyn, who was a wealthy mercer. He was the father of Anne Boleyn, the second wife of King Henry VIII, and through her the maternal grandfather of Queen Elizabeth 1 of England.

Channeled from Anne Boleyn by Penny Genter:

My dearest Penny.

We were catalysts to begin to break the hold of the false church that had been commandeered by evil. The drama that was set into place by the "volunteers" of change was not an easy one, but necessary. Though the instigator, Henry, allowed his own agendas and ego to cast a wide net of horror and destruction, in the end, the course of history was altered, and the run-away train derailed.

As for my part in all of this, I was not without my own lessons in guile and subterfuge. The more I fell under the spell of the family I had chosen for incarnation into, the greater my karmic lessons. We are directed before incarnation to a narrow path, but since we are not all-knowing, perfected beings, it is easy to slip off the predetermined course. That is where the karmic lessons come in.

Though history has not treated me kindly, there is much that was covered up and buried along the way. This will eventually be revealed but is unnecessary for balancing the scales of justice. The lessons were learned, the course of the river diverted, and the town saved.

The path you have chosen in this lifetime is a narrow one, but you have made the necessary course corrections to avoid the rapids. The whole soul group played out important lessons in that time period and should be commended for learning from past "mistakes" and making better choices this time around. In doing so, all have been elevated to a higher path of service.

I am thankful that time is past, and all have learned to work together in peace and harmony in a loving household. Too bad we did not do that then. All is perfect. And so it is...

Anne

Constanze Mozart (1762-1842AD)

Constanze Weber was born in Germany and lived most of her early life in Mannheim, an important cultural, intellectual and musical center. She, her sisters were trained as singers. She married Wolfgang Amadeus Mozart in 1782. They had six children, of whom only two survived infancies. Constanze was a trained musician and played a role in her husband's career.

On 14 December 1784, Mozart became a Freemason[1]. Freemasonry played an important role in the remainder of Mozart's life.

The Illuminati[2] was a masonically inspired group which was founded by a friend of Mozart's. The Illuminati espoused the Enlightenment-inspired, humanist views. The music of the Freemasons contained musical phrases and forms that held specific meanings. there are many other examples of specific musical symbols taken from the Masonic rites that

---

[1]**Freemasonry**, the teachings and practices of the secret fraternal (men-only) order of Free and Accepted Masons, the largest worldwide secret society. Spread by the advance of the British Empire, Freemasonry remains most popular in the British Isles and in other countries originally within the empire. Estimates of the worldwide membership of Freemasonry in the early 21st century ranged from about two million to more than six million. Freemasonry evolved from the guilds of stonemasons and cathedral builders of the Middle Ages. With the decline of cathedral building, some lodges of operative (working) masons began to accept honorary members to bolster membership. The degrees of freemasonry retain the three grades of medieval craft guilds, those of Apprentice, Journeyman or fellow (now called Fellowcraft), and Master Mason.

The traditions of Freemasonry are founded upon the building of King Solomon's Temple, and its fraternal ceremonies use the working tools of the stonemasons to symbolize moral lessons and truths. For example, Masons are reminded at Lodge to "meet upon the level of equality, act by the plumb of uprightness, and part upon the square of virtue."

Modern Freemasonry broadly consists of two main recognition groups. Regular Freemasonry insists that a volume of scripture is open in a working lodge, that every member profess belief in a Supreme Being, that no women are admitted, and that the discussion of religion and politics is banned. Continental Freemasonry is now the general term for the "liberal" jurisdictions which have removed some, or all, of these restrictions.

22[2] The **Illuminati** is a name given to several groups, both real and fictitious. Historically, the name usually refers to the **Bavarian Illuminati**, an Enlightenment-era secret society founded on 1 May 1776. The society's goals were to oppose superstition, obscurantism *(the practice of deliberately presenting information in an imprecise and recondite manner, often*

appear throughout Mozart's compositions including *The Magic Flute*. The Illuminati contended that social rank was not coincident with nobility of the spirit, but that people of lowly class could be noble in spirit just as nobly born could be mean-spirited.

Mozart died in 1791, leaving debts. She obtained a pension from the emperor, organized profitable memorial concerts, and embarked on a campaign to publish the works of her husband. These efforts gradually made Constanze financially secure and ultimately, wealthy.

She sent her boys Karl and Franz to Prague to be educated by Franz Xavier Niemetschek with whom she collaborated on the first full length biography of Mozart. She married George Nikolaus von Nissen a Danish diplomat and writer. Both worked on a biography of Mozart that she published after her second husband's death.

---

designed to forestall further inquiry and understanding, the deliberate restriction of knowledge, opposition to disseminating knowledge and, deliberate obscurity characterized by deliberate vagueness), and religious influence over public life, and abuses of state power. "The order of the day," they wrote in their general statutes, "is to put an end to the machinations of the purveyors of injustice, to control them without dominating them."

The Illuminati—along with Freemasonry and other secret societies—were outlawed through edict by the Bavarian ruler Charles Theodore with the encouragement of the Catholic Church, in 1784, 1785, 1787, and 1790. In the several years following, the group was vilified by conservative and religious critics who claimed that they continued underground and were responsible for the French Revolution.

In subsequent use, "Illuminati" refers to various organizations which claim or are purported to have links to the original Bavarian Illuminati or similar secret societies, though these links are unsubstantiated. They are often alleged to conspire to control world affairs, by masterminding events and planting agents in government and corporations in order to gain political power and influence and to establish a New World Order. Central to some of the most widely known and elaborate conspiracy theories, the Illuminati have been depicted as lurking in the shadows and pulling the strings and levers of power in dozens of novels, films, television shows, comics, video games, and music videos.

Penny –

Having outlived three husbands, I can relate to the struggles of widowhood. Of course, her skills as a writer are something I share as well.

Though I have no developed musical talent in this lifetime, I am enchanted by the work of Mozart. The movie Amadeus opened me to an appreciation that was shielded from me in my early years, but I have made up for lost time. I have watched the movie Amadeus many times.

A good friend in this lifetime is named Amadeus. I believe he was my husband then.

Harry – I "get" that Harry was George Nikolaus von Nisson, Constanza's second husband. Now he is intensely triggered by the Illuminati and Masonic activities.

Teresa -

"I love his work now, and loved his music, and symphonies then.

I mourned for his ill-fated luck at that time.

I was a sponsor of his plays and tried to help him financially. I was able to support him somehow."

Janice – I "get Janice was Mozart's elder sister, Maria Anna (1751–1829), nicknamed "Nannerl". When Nannerl was seven, she began keyboard lessons with her father while her three-year-old brother looked on. Years later, after her brother's death, she reminisced:

He often spent much time at the clavier, picking out thirds, which he was ever striking, and his pleasure showed that it sounded good.... In the fourth year of his age his father, for a game as it were, began to teach him a few minutes and pieces at the clavier.... He could play it faultlessly and with the greatest delicacy and keeping exactly in time.... At the age of five, he was already composing little pieces, which he played to his father who wrote them down.

Maria Anna (Marianne) Mozart was born in Salzburg. When she was seven years old, her father Leopold Mozart started teaching her to play the harpsichord. Leopold took her and Wolfgang on tours of many cities, such as Vienna and Paris, to showcase their talents. In the early days, she sometimes received top billing, and she was noted as an excellent harpsichord player and forte pianist. However, given the views of her parents, prevalent in her society at the time, it became impossible as she grew older for her to continue her career any further. According to *New Grove*, "from 1769 onwards she was no longer permitted to show her artistic talent on travels with her brother, as she had reached a marriageable age.

Wolfgang wrote a number of works for Marianne to perform. There is evidence that Marianne wrote musical compositions, as there are letters from Wolfgang praising her work, but the voluminous correspondence of her father never mentions any of her compositions, and none have survived.

In contrast to her brother, who quarreled with their father and eventually disobeyed his wishes with respect to career path and choice of spouse, Marianne remained entirely subordinate to her father. Eventually, Marianne married a magistrate, Johann von Berchtold, who was twice a widower and had five children from his two previous marriages, whom Marianne helped raise. She also bore three children of her own

John -

I "get" that John was **Johann Georg Leopold Mozart** (November 14, 1719 – May 28, 1787) was a German composer, conductor, teacher, and violinist. Mozart is best known today as the father and teacher of Wolfgang Amadeus Mozart.

James Mitchell Varnum (1748-1789AD)

James Mitchell Varnum was an American legislator, lawyer, and general in the Continental Army during the Revolutionary War. He was one of George Washington's generals at Valley Forge.

At Valley Forge, soldiers deserted in "astonishing great numbers" as hardships at camp overcame their motivation and dedication to fight. General James Mitchell Varnum warned that the desperate lack of supplies would "force the army to mutiny."

The winter at Valley Forge imbued into soldiers a strong will to persevere, endure, and later triumph over obstacles and bring independence to the United States. Washington always acknowledged that the perseverance gained by the soldiers at Valley Forge was what made the Continental Army bind together even stronger and eventually win the war.

In a past-life regression I saw the horrors of that time with mud and frozen bodies everywhere. I felt the impetus to change the situation and therefore the lives of the men under my command.

Penny - *I believe my third husband had a previous incarnation as George Washington.*

In this lifetime we lived on what had been the Mt. Vernon plantation in Virginia owned by George Washington.

The name Mitchell has been a thread that has woven in and out of many of my lifetimes. My father's name was Charles Lawrence Mitchell. He died when I was five and reincarnated as my son Mitchell Lawrence. I find that many reincarnations are in grandchildren or other family lines so that we can complete unfinished business. Of course, Mitchell was my maiden name.

I was waiting for my bags at the luggage carousel at the airport in Hong Kong. Just as I tried to retrieve my overloaded bag, a small boy dove in front of me causing me to twist which herniated several discs in my lower back. I have had trouble and pain in that area for many years since that time. I believe this boy was the reincarnation of a man I had mortally wounded in battle in my lifetime as James Mitchell Varner. I have tracked this and worked consciously to recognize my action in that lifetime, accept responsibility, ask forgiveness, and give thanks, a process known as "ho'oponopono." We may not be able to remove all of the trauma in our life, but we can work to get the lesson so that it does not have to be repeated.

I had one encounter that was jarring. I met a woman and felt an immediate discomfort and distrust of her. She had done nothing in this incarnation, to my knowledge, but the feeling continued. I began tracking and asking questions of my higher self and discovered that she had been a soldier in the army I commanded. The conditions were deplorable at Valley Forge and he(she) had been conscripted and forced to leave behind a pregnant girlfriend. In an effort to escape, he(she) organized a fragging incident where I was injured. The subterfuge was discovered and he(she) was executed.

I prayed on this and forgave him(her) and myself in this and previous lifetimes in order to release the energy that separated us so that we could find a loving path together in this one.

Gordon - I "get" that Gordon had been **George Washington**. Historians laud Washington for the selection and supervision of his generals, preservation and command of the army, coordination with the Congress, with state governors and their militia, and attention to supplies, logistics, and training. In battle, however, Washington was repeatedly outmaneuvered by British generals with larger armies. After victory had been finalized in 1783, Washington resigned as commander-in-chief rather than seize power, proving his opposition to dictatorship and his commitment to American republicanism.

Janice - I "get that Janice was **Brigadier General Anthony Wayne**. To supplement those supplies received from Congress, Washington sent Wayne to New Jersey in February 1778, to gather food and cattle for the men. A month later, Wayne returned with 50 head of cattle and 30 horses. With the arrival of warmer weather in March, disease began strike at the army. Over the next three months, influenza, typhus, typhoid, and dysentery all erupted within the encampment. Of the 2,000 men who died at Valley Forge, over two-thirds were killed by disease. These outbreaks were eventually contained through sanitation regulations, inoculations, and the work of surgeons.

Will – I "get" that Will was **Baron Friederich Wilhelm von Steuben**, a former member of the Prussian General Staff. He had been recruited to the American cause in Paris by Benjamin Franklin. Accepted by Washington, von Steuben was put to work designing a training program for the army. Though he spoke no English, von Steuben commenced his program in March with the aid of interpreters. Beginning with a "model company" of 100 chosen men, von Steuben instructed them in drill, maneuver, and a simplified manual of arms.

These 100 men were in turn sent out to other units to repeat the process and so on until the entire army was trained. In addition, von Steuben introduced a system of progressive training for recruits which educated them in the basics of soldiering.

Dave – I "get" that Dave was once again on the opposing side as an officer in the British Army. **Charles Cornwallis, 1st Marquis Cornwallis** (1738 – 1805) was a British Army officer and colonial administrator. In the United States and the United Kingdom. He is best remembered as one of the leading British generals in the American War of Independence. His surrender in 1781 to a combined American and French force at the Siege of Yorktown ended significant hostilities in North America.

Bo – I "get" that once again Bo was a soldier under my command.

Jewels – I "get" that my current friend Jewels was in that lifetime a soldier under my command who had a problem with alcohol. One day I came upon him passed out on the floor drunk. I went to poke him in the shoulder to awaken him with my sword and he startled awake, severely cutting the shoulder. This became infected and had to be amputated.

In this lifetime I suffered from chronic shoulder pain. I kept getting that it sourced back to this lifetime. I kept getting the word 'miasma' which I remembered from working with the Perelandra Flower Essences and reading the work of Machaelle Small Wright.

In Greek mythology, a **miasma** is "a contagious power ... that has an independent life of its own. Until purged by the sacrificial death of the wrongdoer, society would be chronically infected by catastrophe." I decided to ask Archangel Raphael for insight into this dis-ease and its ramifications in multiple lifetimes.

My dearest Penny,

You are right in your connection of addictions with their underlying root in the soul memories of individuals. While not necessarily as well-known as familial connection, there is a more deep-rooted source within the soul stream that continues to confront this challenge until the root causes are addressed.

Early physicians and health care providers realized that there was something causing dis-ease but could not identify the causative factor. They gave it the name miasma and wrongly deduced that it must be air-born since they could not see a physical connection.

While "modern" science has moved on in their effort to categorize and explain disease, the root causes of the addictive urge, ***the causative factor, is sourced in soul memories****. Somewhere in the progression from lifetime to lifetime the soul developed an anomaly that attached to the soul that incarnates time and again into future incarnations searching for understanding and amelioration. While different "mechanical" and self-discipline methods can be utilized to control the urges and allow the expression of the soul's purpose in a lifetime, the miasma of addiction remains buried, as does that of tuberculosis, until it emerges again in future incarnations.*

As to what can be done to remove this propensity from the soul stream, we might suggest that various techniques for soul regression have proved effective. This may require an outside assistant if the subject is not sufficiently conscious and can guide themselves through a process of awareness, intention to learn the lesson and let it go, forgiveness of self and others, love, gratitude, and release. Once this negative block is removed from the soul path, it should no longer resurface in future incarnations.

You might wish to look at this as a slippery slope. When you choose to take this seeming shortcut rather than the steeper route of awareness, introspection, integrity, self-love, and honor, there are many pitfalls along the way that will affect not only your progress today but, in your lives, to come. Stepping off this treacherous path and studying the roadmaps that got you here and where you wish to be allows you to leave the lessons well-learned behind and move forward, free of the burdens that impeded your progress.

We hope this gives you a clearer vision of what can be done by those resolute in changing their route to sobriety.

AA Raphael

Leopoldine Hugo (1824-1843AD)

Leopoldine Cecile Marie Pierre Catherine Hugo was the eldest daughter of novelist, poet and dramatist Victor Hugo and his wife, Adele Foucher. She married Charles Vacquerie but they both drowned together only a few months later when their boat capsized on the Seine. She died when her wet, heavy skirts pulled her down and her husband died trying to save her. This tragic event had a great impact on the work and personality of her father Victor Hugo. He dedicated numerous poems to the memory of his daughter. The character of the orphan Cocotte adopted by Jean Val Jean in ***Les Misérables*** was a tribute to the daughter of Victor Hugo who died.

Jami I "get" that Jami was **Charles Vacquerie**, Leopoldine's husband who drowned trying to save her.

> "I to this day have an aversion to petticoats, slips and stacks of female under layer clothing. I feel disdain when I see women's clothing from the past that are tightly fitting wool monstrosities. I repel against tight clothing and fashions that cover one from neck to toes. Even my mother used to chase me out of the house as I headed to school to make sure I had a proper slip on under my clothes... I tried everything to get away without her noticing! I am certainly happy to be a female in today's world-- free to be eclectic and petticoat free! (Sorry Penny that I couldn't save you in that life. Life seemed pretty cushy here and we might rather have had more relaxing time before incarnating in another surge of chaos!)"

Victor Hugo – 26 February 1802 – 22 May 1885) was a French poet, novelist, and dramatist of the Romantic movement. Hugo is considered to be one of the greatest and best-known French writers. Outside of France, his most famous works are the novels **Les Miserables**, 1862, and ***The Hunchback of Notre-Dane*** (French: *Notre-Dame de Paris*), 1831.

I have been obsessed with the story of *Les Misérables* since I first saw the musical in 1985. I have seen it many times including the movies and have read much of the huge book. Many of the people I know in this lifetime I recognize as being characters in the drama whose theme is hope and redemption.

Graham Simmans (1919-2005)

A future incarnation of Victor Hugo, Graham Simmans was an Archeologist in Egypt, who helped unearth the Nag Hammadi scrolls and lived in Rennes le Chateau. I was led to his book ***Jesus after the Crucifixion*** in the bookstore at Rennes la Chateau. I followed that with ***REX Deus*** which he wrote with Henry Lincoln who I met later. Both books resonated with me. He had passed over the same week as my husband. I got that they were both working on the other side with the White Brotherhood.

He came to me in a channeling and asked me to go back to Rennes le Chateau. He suggested that I contact Ani who I knew of but had not yet met. I e-mailed her that Graham Simmans had asked me to contact her. She e-mailed me back and said that we needed to talk – She had lived in Graham Simmans' house in Rennes la Chateau for three years! I went back to Rennes le Chateau with Ani in 2010 on an amazing pilgrimage to many of the places we had been guided by Spirit two years earlier.

(Author note – A soul can operate in many different time lines at the same time because Spirit knows no boundary with time. Sometimes two aspects of the same soul need to be incarnated at the same time to get more of the soul's work done.)

Teresa **-** *Victor Hugo*

> *"He was my Hero in this life time, I read books of his when I was at the convent, as a student of middle school. My favorite was The Lady of the Camellias, - I become one with her. Revolting in this way to the stupid rules imposed on me by the nuns. I wanted to grow to be a prostitute. Hum ...De ja vu?*
>
> *Also, I felt the pain of losing what I knew prior to being in the convent.*

Les Misérables, I felt what itis to lose everything and have the knot on your throat of losing everything dear to me. It was a very dark cycle in my life and I was not prepared to handle. So again, I gravitated to you, and a group recognizing familiarity. I explained to you earlier about soul group feelings – what one learns, impacts all."

Bo – I "get" that Bo was Victor Hugo's childhood friend **Adèle Foucher** (1803–1868). Because of his close relationship with his mother, Hugo waited until after her death (in 1821) to marry Adèle in 1822. They had four children including Victor's favorite Leopoldine. That would have made him my mother.

Honore de Balzac 1799-1850

French novelist and playwright. Friend of Victor Hugo. Hugo's protagonist of Jean Val Jean in Les Misérables, a former prisoner that was redeemed, was patterned upon his friend, Honore de Balzac.

My good friend, housemate for five years, and author Don I believe, is a reincarnation of de Balzac. He has dedicated his life to redemption of prisoners.

Don

*- I have gone back over that entry in your manuscript and am fine with it. I certainly do relate well with the character Jean Val Jean, so who knows... perhaps **Balzac** and I do have more in common than I would have thought. Writing and prison reform are my two most driving passions in this lifetime, as far as I can tell.*

Joy

We lived near Victor as sisters and interacted with him almost on a daily basis. We watched his children and game them baths. He was a remarkable man and we helped him and his family a lot.

Paul L'hote (1841-1921AD) (the Impressionist period)

Of all my previous lifetimes, the one I spent in the company of the Impressionists in France seems to be the most strongly imprinted in this one. For my whole life I have been drawn to beauty of this transformative period of art. From the art history classes, interior and landscape design degrees, to the classes I taught on French Impressionist Gardens, this is a theme that runs through this lifetime. My home is filled with French Impressionist art and design. The many times I have visited Paris and been called to the Impressionist museums and the streets of Montmartre recall an epoch that permeates my life today and seems to be a lesson I am still learning.

I believe many of those I count in my circle of friends today were also incarnated in this pivotal period of history. I have identified many of them. In that lifetime we began the exploration of relationship which is flowering in understanding in this one.

In the book ***Occult Paris: The Lost Magic of the Belle-Époque*** by Tobias Churton, he says that during Paris's Belle Époque (1871-1914), many cultural movements and artistic styles flourished--Symbolism, **Impressionism**, Art Nouveau, the Decadents--all of which profoundly shaped modern culture. **Paris became the locus for the most intense revival of magical practices and doctrines since the Renaissance**. Exploring the magical, artistic, and intellectual world of the Belle Époque, a wide variety of Theosophists, **Rosicrucians,** Martinists, Freemasons, Gnostics, and neo-Cathars called Paris home. Cultural advancement was the explosion of occult activity taking place in the City of Light at the same time.

Churton talks about the richness of the Hermetic movements of the time, mostly in Paris, and also a bit in the **Languedoc** region where it eventually extended to. These schools of thought were nothing original per se, if you consider the multitude of esoteric movements that sprung throughout French history (for instance the **Cathars**).

The 19th century in France was quite chaotic, with two empires, two monarchies, and three republics. It was a time of cultural, social, and political crisis. The artists' aspiration to spiritual life was part of a reaction to the new, scientific, and materialistic theories and development and the demolition of the past through the modernization of Paris.

Art history was a spiritual revolution. Many so-called Impressionist painters of the time should more correctly be called Symbolists, with their art referring to something beyond the domain of the visible. This occult enthusiasm was a common thread throughout Europe, as materialism encroached further in the wake of mass production and mechanized warfare amid the unnerving consequences of Darwinian evolution theory and geology's explosion of the biblical time frame. They set themselves against the superficial aspects of their age, and nostalgic for times lost, they desired to trace a way through the ugliness of their times.

These people were all concerned with the synthesis of the arts of word, painting, music, and drama (like Wagner, whom many revered), and how **art had the power of connecting visible and invisible worlds**. For them, the artist was an initiate, a visionary, a prophet. Hence, they considered Paris a center of gnosis.

We are mostly dealing with a kind of "esoteric Christianity" that aimed at transcending the world's gross material grip (with echoes from the Cathar message= Neo-Catharism). This is about a search for mysticism, for inner knowledge. Inspired by past spiritual guides (e.g. Giordano Bruno, Hermes Trismegistus), they were seeking a primordial tradition of knowledge, an enchantment, a way to the depths, to mystery and meaning, to gnosis, through symbolism and art.

Because we are here in the presence of "a Hermetic spiritual movement dedicated not to theological or exclusively philosophical doctrines, but to the transformative power of the arts of the imagination. Most of these artists were led to abstract art, for the sake of The Ideals. Those belonging to these groups could actually be very practical in form, with some fraternities even involving medical care freely offered, and the organization of yearly art exhibits (salons), periodicals, and lectures, for the sake of education. These salons' aim was to "insufflate theocratic essence into contemporary art", to oppose the materialism represented by the erection of an iron (Eifel) tower much opposed by many writers and artists of the time.

Churton's work shows the multiplicity and variety of schools, with different perspectives, goals, and practices. Some had connections with Kabbalistic (use of numerology and the golden section in La Mer and other works by Debussy) and Masonic Orders. But they all had in common a denial of positivist materialism. Some actually even aspired to reconcile faith and science.

The Rosicrucian tradition dates back to the mystery schools of ancient Egypt during the Eighteenth Dynasty, around 1500 BCE. In those schools, whose existence is now recognized by most historians and Egyptologists, Initiates gathered to study the mysteries of creation; hence the word "mysticism", literally meaning "study of the mysteries." Over time, that study gave birth to a gnosis which was transmitted to Ancient Greece, the Roman Empire, Europe of the Middle Ages, and finally received by the Rosicrucians of the seventeenth century.

Rosicrucianism is a spiritual and cultural movement which arose in Europe in the early 17th century after the publication of several texts which purported to announce the existence of a hitherto unknown esoteric order to the world and made seeking its knowledge attractive to many. The mysterious doctrine of the order is allegedly "built on esoteric truths of the ancient past", which "concealed from the average man, provide insight into nature, the physical universe, and the spiritual realm." The manifestos do not elaborate extensively on the matter, but clearly combine references to Kabbalah, Hermeticism, alchemy, and mystical Christianity.

According to Masonic writers, the Order of the Rose Cross is expounded in a major Christian literary work that molded the subsequent spiritual beliefs of western civilization: *The Divine Comedy* (ca.1808-1821) by Dante Alighieri.

The Roseline or Paris Meridian of the Da Vinci Code fame runs through the church of San Sulpice in Paris and continues through Rennes-le-Chateau.

Many of the soul group surrounding the Impressionists and incarnate in Sedona today were part of the Rosicrucians who met in and around Saint Sulpice in Paris. This was a center of learning and metaphysical study that was blossoming at that time. They channeled Galileo, Francis Bacon, and others in search of higher truths.

Before the veil came down in 1892, the Seminary of Saint Sulpice had been the center of learning, stimulated by curiosity and discovery. After the discovery of documents at Rennes-le-Chateau, Abbé' Berenger Saunier brought the documents he had discovered in his church to Saint Sulpice for investigation. Cannon Lilley was called to Paris to look at the documents and stated that they provided "**incontrovertible evidence that Jesus was alive in 45 A.D.**" The documents are presumed to be in the Vatican archives. The Vatican has a history of obtaining- and destroying- writings that run counter to the myth it is promulgating as true history.

In 1902, Pope Leo XIII created the Pontifical Biblical Commission to monitor and direct Catholic theological scholarship. It opposed modernism, the work of those scholars around the Seminary of Saint Sulpice in Paris before such teaching was condemned late in the nineteenth century. During the nineteenth century the Modernists wished to revise the dogmatic assertions of church teachings in the light of discoveries made by science, archaeology, and critical scholarship. In 1910 all priests and Catholic teachers were required to swear an oath against Modernism. Students at seminaries and theological colleges were forbidden to read newspapers. In an attempt to halt the spread of knowledge, the railways were banned by the Pope for fear that travel and communication would harm religion.

I believe we are being brought back to remember the beauty, courage, intuition, joy and camaraderie we experienced in that lifetime, before we were punished for enjoying life by distorted religious programming. We are turning back on the memories of life being lived in abundance, beauty, and fearlessly by knowing our true selves and the endless possibilities life affords when we choose to courageously be our divine selves. As we are blessed, we also bless others as we allow the abundance to flow through us to those in need.

The Luncheon of the Boating Party by Pierre-August Renoir

In 2006 I was awakened in the night and told to get a book off my shelf about Renoir that I had bought a few years before at the Renoir exhibit in Boston. When I began exploring the painting of *the Luncheon of the Boating Party*, I first learned of the man who I was in that lifetime – Paul L'hote, (the man in the straw hat leering at the woman in the upper right corner) an amateur painter and close friend of Renoir and the other impressionists. This became a roadmap for the next phase of my life's journey.

The Impressionists were masters of Light. New technologies of paint in tubes allowed them to move out of the studio and into nature where the natural world shown in all its glory. They threw off shackles of the establishment and painted ordinary people in their daily lives rather than the heroic, religious, and rigid themes that were required in the past.

Most of the Impressionist painters struggled initially until America first saw the value in the impressionist works and created a new market that soon spread back to Europe. Eventually the artists began to move higher in circumstance and reap the rewards of their labors. Many of the movers and shakers in this time were wealthy and others aspired to the lifestyle. They partied and lived life lavishly, eschewing religious programming and vows that berated that life style.

They became **Alchemists of Light working in the Field.**

I recently found on-line a portrait of Renoir that I, as Paul L'hote, had painted. We painted, traveled, partied and grew together as we exchanged our techniques, perceptions and visions of a lifetime in transition. Renoir, especially, was a magnificent portrait painter. All of the impoverished impressionists painted their friends and associates as well as the movers and shakers of the time, so we have a visual record of much of that period. They were great letter writers and have left important insights to the stories behind the paintings.

I frequently appeared in his paintings including the *Dance in the Country* with his future wife, Aline Charigot who is my friend Amara in this lifetime.

Amara and I knew we had to visit site of our past lives so in 2008 we were led on a spirit-guided tour of France and explored many of the sites of our Impressionist lifetimes. We stayed in Montmartre where we had lived and immersed ourselves in the place and the time. We were blown away by the Muse d-Orsay, the Impressionist museum in Paris. We visited Monet's home and garden in Giverny, Cezanne's home and garden in Aix-en-Provence, and Renoir's home and garden in Cagnes. With every step we seemed drawn more deeply in that life that we had shared.

There are books written about the painting that give insight into the characters including *Luncheon of the Boating Party* by Susanne Vreeland. As I connected these faces with the people in my life I saw many similarities in the faces and traits that I recognized in our current incarnation. Two of my husbands, two former lovers, a couple of close friends and companions, and two writers I am particularly drawn to were all part of the soul group pictured on the balcony we were later to visit. I became "obsessed" in finding our connection then and now and what this was showing me through the distorted prism of my understanding.

In that lifetime I was a life-long bachelor and lover of the ladies. I was a journalist, a wild-adventurer who had at one time fought a duel, and seeker of truth. Though I seem to have learned lessons of bravado in that lifetime, I continue to be drawn to the written word as evidenced by my several books.

The first relationship we enter into is frequently a karmic one. Karmic relationships often are those lessons that we were unable to learn in a previous lifetime—these people aren't meant to take it easy on us, because they are meant to change our way of life. That was certainly true of my first husband who, after giving me four children to raise, was murdered in a senseless killing, allowing me to feel the consequences of my previous life actions. Several of the women I was romantically involved with in that lifetime have shown up as men in this one with harsh lessons to balance karma. It has been when I am able to consciously track and dissect the lessons of painful or significant relationships in this one that I am frequently drawn back to my unfinished business as Paul Lhote! I am thankful to have finally "gotten it", loved it, and moved on.

I began putting together paintings, mostly by Renoir, with people I knew in this lifetime, both in Albuquerque/Santa Fe and Sedona. Striking physical resemblances were evident and even more when I began matching up characteristics I was reading about with the people I knew in my life. I put these together in a presentation I did at Unity and others began to realize the soul group that was coming back together.

Amara - The seamstress **Aline Charigot**, who is holding a dog, sits near the bottom left of the composition. Renoir married her in 1890, and they had three sons.

Gordon – I "get" that my late husband Gordon was Actress **Ellen Andree** who drinks from a glass in the center of the composition. André was born in 1857 in Paris. She started her work as a model and she has become notable because she appeared in a number of important impressionist paintings. She was an actress in the Naturalist style of theatre where the purpose was to give a near perfect view of real scenes and not to rely on the audience's imagination. She was a star mime at the Follies –Bergere. She appeared in plays and comedies and worked for several decades as an actress, but it was the brief period in the 1870s when she was a model for a number of artists but importantly Edouard Manet, Edgar Degas, and Pierre-Auguste Renoir that made her name notable.

Will – I "get" that Will was actress **Jeanne Samary**. While enjoying success and recognition as a comedic actress, Jeanne hoped for more substantial and prestigious roles. She did not want to be eternally characterized as "stout, pink, and merry" as the newspapers described her in her maid's costume.

In order to advance her career, Jeanne began working as a model. Her ambition appears to have been to be painted in the same style as Sarah Bernhardt, in order to attract the same type of dramatic, tragic roles which received greater respect.

She attracted the attention of the newly famous Renoir, always an aficionado of beautiful young women (particularly curvaceous strawberry blondes). Alas for the ambitious Samary and the only recently lauded Renoir, both works were derided for the critics for their sketchy brushstrokes and intentionally patchy light, and neither served to launch her as a notable beauty. At some point around 1877, Samary almost certainly became Renoir's lover.

Derek – I "get" that in that lifetime Derek was **Eugene Pierre Lestringez**, an occultist and best friend of Paul L'hote. Renoir depicts them flirting with the actress Jeanne Samary in the upper right-hand corner of the painting. He worked in the Ministry of the Interior and in his spare time indulged his passion for the occult by hypnotizing his friends.

I have not yet met Derek in this lifetime though I know his work well as it mirrors my own interests. I was attracted to his books on photography 30 years ago and those on impressionist gardens were reference books for the classes I taught at the University of New Mexico. He was inspirational in my visiting Monet, Cezanne, and Renoir's gardens. Friendship transcends lifetimes...

Bo – I "get" that Bo was **Gustave Caillebotte**. In the right foreground, Gustave Caillebotte wears a white boater's shirt and flat-topped straw boater's hat as he sits backwards in his chair. I am astounded by the physical resemblance of Caillebotte and the Bo I know today.

Gustave Caillebotte (1848 – 1894) was a French painter, member and patron of the artists known as Impressionists, although he painted in a much more realistic manner than many other artists in the group. Caillebotte was noted for his early interest in photography as an art form. Caillebotte was also an avid boatman, yacht builder, and drew on that subject for several works. Caillebotte's sizable allowance, along with the inheritance he received after the death of his father in 1874 and his mother in 1878, allowed him to paint without the pressure to sell his work. It also allowed him to help fund Impressionist exhibitions and support his fellow artists and friends (including Claude Monet, Auguste Renoir, and Camille Pissarro among others) by purchasing their works and, at least in the case of Monet, paying the rent for their studios. He and Monet shared a love of gardening and exchanged ideas and techniques. He collected works of all the impressionists and after his death bequeathed them and many of his own works to the Louvre. This eventually became the foundation for the enormously popular Impressionist collection.

Caillebotte was a Rosicrucian, master at perspective, sacred geometry and imbedding sacred symbols in his work.

Gene - I "get" that my second husband, Gene, was **Alphonse Fournaise, Jr**., sporting traditional straw boater hat and appearing to the left side of the image. Alphonse, who was responsible for the boat rental, is the leftmost figure. His father owned the restaurant where this was painted.

Gene's father owned a restaurant.

Kathleen – I "get" that Kathleen was **Adrien Maggiolo**, an Italian Journalist for *Le Triboulet*, no surprise given her current life as a writer and researcher.

Teresa -

I "get" that Teresa was **Alfred Sisley**, one of the Impressionist painters.

Renoir always loved the South part of France.
I feel at home with Renoir, Monet, Cezanne.
I also feel much closer to Lautrec. Perverted, a dwarf but ....
something very familiar.

Janice -

"I am a "closet artist" myself, (not showing any of my artwork), but won the art award in high school. When I lived in Washington DC, I would often go to the art galleries there. I did calligraphy work for President Johnson's daughter Lynda when she got married. Of course, Renoir's painting of "Luncheon of the Boating Party" is there, where we also have a connection:

I was ***Charles Ephrussi****, the man Renoir painted standing, my back turned and speaking to a younger man. Not surprising that I was an art connoisseur, critic, and collector. I have many other lifetimes as an artist in various modalities: painting, sculpture, calligraphy, glass & pottery. I was a great friend of Marcel Proust (I was used as a model in his writings) and in this lifetime, the "love of my life", a man named Victor, was Proust. Victor and I have shared many artistic lifetimes together."*

Dave I "get" that in that lifetime Dave was **Jeanne Elizabeth Schmahl** (1846–1915) a French feminist, born in Britain. She married a well-off husband who supported her while she worked as a midwife's assistant in Paris. She decided to avoid politics and religion and to focus on specific and practical feminist goals. She led a successful campaign to change the laws, so women could legally bear witness and could control their own earnings. She launched the French Union for Women's Suffrage to campaign for the right of women to vote, but that was not achieved in her lifetime.

Dave is a former state senator

Nancy – I "get" that Nancy was **Jean-François Millet** (1814 – 1875) was a French painter and one of the founders of the Barbizon school in rural France. Millet is noted for his scenes of peasant farmers; he can be categorized as part of the Realism art movement.

In this lifetime Nancy spent time in France photographing a book on French peasant farmers.

I "get" that Nancy was also a woman Van Gogh was infatuated with in San Remy.

> *"I have always loved the earth and remember when*
> *I painted heart-warming scenes of men and women*
> *caring for the great mother in all her seasons. I*
> *loved the simplicity and contact each made while*
> *nurturing the soil, the plants and the trees. New*
> *colors were discovered in these precious moments.*
> *This memory has always been with me, in my heart,*
> *especially as I lived with and documented the last of*
> *the French peasant farmers, as a photojournalist,*
> *early in my career during this lifetime."*

Jim I "get" that Jim was Paul L'hotse's daughter.

John –

I "get" that John was **Eugène Henri Paul Gauguin** (7 June 1848 – 8 May 1903) a French post-Impressionist artist. Unappreciated until after his death, Gauguin is now recognized for his experimental use of color and Synthetist style that were distinctly different from Impressionism. Towards the end of his life he spent ten years in French Polynesia, and most of his paintings from this time depict people or landscapes from that region.

His work was influential to the French avant-garde and many modern artists, such as Pablo Picasso and Henri Matisse. Gauguin was an important figure in the Symbolist movement as a painter, sculptor, printmaker, ceramist, and writer.

John confirms that his facial characteristics certainly resemble Gauguin's. John has a long-life career as a professional artist and teacher of fine art. He says, "my color harmonies certainly remind me of his explorations." While Gauguin abandoned his wife and children, John is a consummate family man and father extraordinaire.

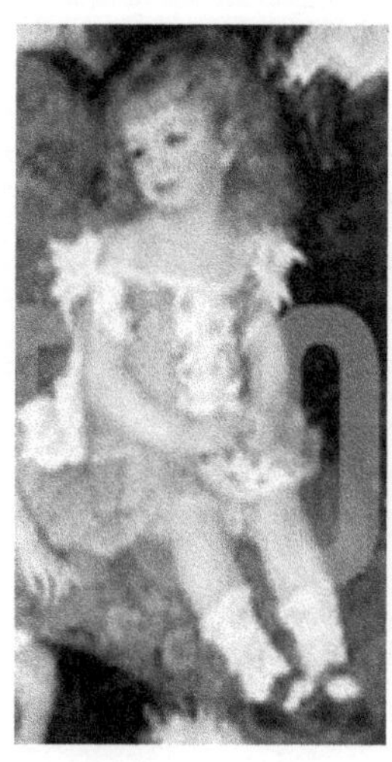

Jami -

"I was a little girl at this time when you were Paul L'hote. I have a sense that this was a gentle life in which I lived in opulence with my sister, who is a close female friend to this day. I had a luxury life, which was a reward for many struggling life times before that, but I feel the most important thing was that I was able to be educated with "Spiritualism," reconnecting with some esoteric and mystery school teachings that had been hidden in the world for a time. I don't think I lived past the age of 16, but my soul needed to remember a comfort in my femininity and needed a life to refresh itself and spent time in the rewards of a civil society blooming with music and art and social connection."

Harry couldn't take his eyes off the picture. Something about it spoke to him in a deep way. After further investigation we discovered that he was Jean Monet with his mother in the painting.

Margaret –

Again, not much has come through except affirmation that I was the companion and second wife of Claude Monet. I helped raise the children after the death of his first wife. I visited France as a teenager and loved the Musee de Orsay which house many impressionist paintings of his garden at Giverny and beautiful gardens and landscapes in general. Perhaps it is what drew me to landscape architecture as a profession in this life.

One of my children in the Monet lifetime is the same friend that was a son in my Yeshua in India life.

Joy –

Penny and I were both amateur painters during this time. We knew all the famous artists by then and were both in the famous painting by the water.

Penny –

I awoke with an intense, stabbing pain in a muscle in my left waist/hip with no apparent cause. After treating it for several hours without relief, I began asking it questions. I "got" that this was related to a past-life experience calling for resolution. I traced it back to my life as Paul L'Hote.

An incident is described in detail in Susan Vreeland's book, Luncheon of the Boating Party. Paul L'Hote, best friend of Renoir, was a journalist and wrote a satiric piece for the paper that described an unnamed woman at a masked ball at Mardi Gras. Her lover, Robert Douvaz thought it to be about his mistress, was offended, and challenged Paul to a duel. Failing to resolve the situation by dialogue, Paul agreed to the use of swords. After some back and forth Paul struck a blow to the opponent just above the hip which is where I currently have the pain. Douvaz was wounded but survived.

I believe that Douvaz is my sister in this lifetime. Though we have an apparent loving relationship now, there was obviously some amends still that needed to be made. I began a process of Ho'oponopono – ***"I am sorry, please forgive me, I love you, thank you****", throughout the day along with Reiki. Within three days my back was back to normal. As I found out in my journey with breast cancer, two of the biggest components of healing are* ***forgiveness*** *and* ***gratitude*** *along with* ***Reiki.***

German Jewish boy. (1932-1938AD)

My parents were militant Jews and members of the Socialist Democratic Party. They were arrested and sent to the Dachau Concentration Camp where I was separated from them. I starved to death at Dachau.

Established in 1863, the SPD is the oldest extant political party represented in the German Parliament and was one of the first Marxist-influenced parties in the world. Adolph Hitler prohibited the party in 1933 under the Enabling Act – party officials were imprisoned, killed or went into exile. In exile, the party used the name Sopade.

Being the only party in the Reichstag to have voted against the Enabling Act (with the Communist Party of Germany prevented from voting), The Enabling Act gave Hitler plenary (full) powers. It followed on the heels of the Reichstag Fire Decree, which abolished most civil liberties and transferred state powers to the Reich government. The combined effect of the two laws was to transform Hitler's government into a de facto legal dictatorship. The SPD was banned in the summer of 1933 by the new Nazi government. Many of its members were jailed or sent to Nazi concentration camps. An exile organization, known as Sopade, was established, initially in Prague. Others left the areas where they had been politically active and moved to other towns where they were not known.

The SPD was outlawed soon after the Nazis came to power in 1933. However, in 1945, with the fall of Adolph Hitler's Third Reich, the SPD was revived.

Penny –

Though at six years old I probably did not have time to accumulate much karma, I am sure though that this was an opportunity to balance many scales. I believe my sense of justice has many roots in this incarnation. I know I have been strongly triggered by incidences of shunning and exclusion and have been outspoken in my criticism of it. Growing up in the civil rights era, I was unusually moved by the struggles I witnessed growing up in the south. Perhaps many of the activists of the 60's and 70's witnessed and experienced the injustices of their previous incarnation and were coming back to do things differently.

I am unusually agitated when I am hungry and find it difficult to fast for even a short period of time. It is something I carry in my cellular memory.

Dr. Brian Weiss found that "People close to starvation, such as those who died in the Holocaust, often become overweight when reincarnated, needing the weight as reassurance they would never be hungry again."

I have no desire to visit Germany today.

Teresa -

"I was 12 when I died at Dachau.
Our families where very close. We worshiped at the Temple and invited each other's families for gatherings.
When the Nazis invaded my home, they wounded me for trying to run. That wound got infected. We stayed together while they sorted out who was who. Without medical attention the wound festered.
When we arrived at Dachau we stayed together at the children dorm as I recognized you.
I shared what I could when I could not swallow any more. I was taken to be executed and I left you behind.
Rebirth for both of us was almost right away with some rest as we died without karma.
Today I distrust soldiers with arms, I consider them bullies, and evil as their excuse to kill is. Just following orders."

Jeff I "get" that Jeff was a friend of my fathers and was sent to Dachau with us

Bo - I "get" that in that lifetime Bo was a Nazi, drawn by the rhetoric and ideals of the leaders. When confronted with the realities of war that went against his deeper knowing, he became disillusioned and joined in the plot to kill Hitler.

Amara – I "get" that in that lifetime Amara was Bo's wife.

Dave – I "get" that in that lifetime Dave was **Alfried Krupp**. The Krupp family, a prominent 400-year-old German dynasty have become famous for their production of steel, artillery, ammunition, and other armaments. The family business, known as Friedrich Krupp AG, was the largest company in Europe at the beginning of the 20th century. It was important to weapons development and production in both world wars. The choices of the Krupp family and firm during the Nazi era, including support of Hitler and use of forced labor, are part of the legacy

Alfried took over full control of the firm, continuing its role as main arms supplier to Germany at war. In 1943, During the war, Krupp was allowed to take over many industries in occupied nations. This activity became the basis for the charge of "plunder" at the war crimes trial of Krupp executives after the war.

As another war crime, Krupp used slave labor, both POWs and civilians from occupied countries, and Krupp representatives were sent to concentration camps to select laborers. Jews were targeted for "extermination through labor". Convinced that Germany would lose the war, he secretly began liquidating 200 million Marks in government bonds. This allowed him to retain much of his fortune and hide it overseas.

Alfried was held in Landsberg prison, where Hitler had been imprisoned in 1924. At the Krupp Trial, held in 1947–1948 in Nuremberg following the main Nuremberg trials, Alfried and most of his co-defendants were convicted of crimes against humanity (plunder and slave labor), while being acquitted of crimes against peace, and conspiracy. Alfried was condemned to 12 years in prison and the "forfeiture of all [his] property both real and personal," making him a pauper. Two years later, on January 31, 1951, John J. McCloy, High Commissioner of the American zone of occupation, issued an amnesty to the Krupp defendants. Much of Alfried's industrial empire was restored, but he was forced to transfer some of his fortune to his siblings, and he renounced arms manufacturing.

Jami –

> *"I had lives during both world wars. In world war 1, I remember being a young woman pregnant with the child of a soldier who held me captive. Another woman was also there in some sort of the same role. I have faint memory (literally) of war experimenting with DNA, and my baby was "cut out" of me early and I died in the process. My brother in this life was the "father" soldier and his wife is the other woman, whom he met on a business trip to Germany 10 years ago. Their daughter*

is the baby that was taken from me. They have a happy marriage. I felt extremely protective over their daughter when I first met her. My brother has been a difficult personality for the family at times, causing family to "walk on egg shells" when around him. This life time was one of many that contributed to karmic balancing with my birth family.

In world war II, I have memory of again being a young woman held as an experimental subject within the personal home of a Nazi scientist. A couple of years ago, I was a housemate with this person for a few months. He saw me in the kitchen one morning and seemed faint when he saw me. I asked if he was ok and stated he was fine considering I chased him with a knife thru his dreams all night! I found that interesting because I had stacked furniture up against my bedroom door every night I had been living there as something in me distrusted him. I saw in a memory that I had indeed "surprised" him and taken his life by knife to end my suffering. I then took my own life.

I sat with him and shared what I saw. I had indeed harmed him, and that energy was coming to him again in his dream, and that I was sorry and asked forgiveness. I also shared that I had been stacking furniture against my door and night and that I forgave the situation now too, grateful we had a new timeline opportunity to look after each other with kindness instead of weirdness. He apologized to me also and we had a sweet hug and a cheerful cup of coffee together to celebrate "the new us." We hid the knives for a few days as a joke and I stopped stacking furniture against my door at night. I continue to see how we indeed cycle together with soul mates, soul family and ancestral family for the continuation of living, loving, learning and forgiving.

I don't recall knowing Penny in any of these life times, although I may have been in genetic experimentation programs in similar times as she was. In another German timeline, I was a part of a life with our current Sedona housemate, Dave. I was in Germany as his big sister and felt responsible for him after our parents were killed. I was unsuccessful in being able to persuade him to stop involvement with a regime that I knew was dangerous. I felt he was getting involved with something that he would not be able to get out of. I "get" that I lost my life as a young woman because I knew too much and had to be silenced. I have many multiple life times as a female in Dave's past lives that made me "worry" about him and what he was getting into or worry about me and what trouble he would get me into! In this life time I have had to become aware of and heal the emotions and feelings I had towards him at times that stemmed from previous life time experiences. I have come to balance to see him as my loving brother and friend in my soul family.

And there is more to the German story. Recently, in this life, I never felt comfortable with traveling to Germany. I didn't even like the word "Germany" and felt uncomfortable when I heard people speaking German. Just this year, I fell in love with a German man doing business in America. As things bloomed in the relationship, he invited me to "meet the parents" on a last-minute trip to Germany to celebrate and surprise his father for his 80th birthday. I felt excitement to spend time with my new sweetheart and meet his family, but.... Germany. Really, oh no! I had a past life regression healing session to help me clear my angst about Germany and to help me clear the time lines I hadn't yet made peace with from my past German life times. Outstanding within this regression was that I had a gruesome death in an incident that officials felt I failed my mission to confiscate weapons. I over estimated my skills in delivering weapons and was put in a damned if I did and damned if I didn't situation. The person who commanded my death was my German sweetheart's German father's brother just 20 miles from where the family lived in Germany. When I was able to clear the charge from this incident and rescue a soul aspect of myself still trapped in that timeline, I was able to shed all the angst for Germany and I had a delightful, loving and beautiful trip to Germany.

I do see how we indeed cycle together with soul mates, soul family and ancestral family for the continuation of living, loving and learning. I had recently seen that for many of us, the world wars were for opportunities for karmic balancing. Many of us came to be "victims" for balance of times we felt we unjustly harmed others, or because someone we dearly loved wanted the "balancing" redemptive opportunity and asked us (from theater side) to come into that life and play the role of our antagonist or perpetrator to help us. Because of love, it seems in some sense we can at times hold up our own evolution to help another. But it's not really a hold up when Love is the reason. It may look like suffering on the front lines of our human experience, but there is always more to "re-member."

Truly, this work is important to embrace as it helps us gain compassion for all sides of the stories of our soul paths and timelines. We have been it all--as the shadow is equal with the light in this dimension for learning. Loving into what we once rejected about ourselves or persecuted others for, we advance to higher consciousness and awareness and begin to operate in a 4th dimensional reality where we can stop floundering on the karmic wheel. We can then begin to love ourselves and everyone for all that we been doing and learning and commit to kindness of ourselves and to others. We stop the seemingly "never-ending" stories and experiences or action/reaction and remorse to play out balance over and over.

For me, I have experienced true forgiveness and unconditional love is easy, natural and complete when I can see/feel compassion for all of us within the experience at the time and embrace my shadow and others. From that space, I call in the Light. My heart is open for the healing to stream thru my timelines and into the hearts of those involved. I come to love for all of us and gain the wisdom from what I was teaching myself or felt called to experience within the situations.

I believe we are here to extend Love to everyone and everything, and this especially means to the shadows of ourselves where we have most rejected ourselves and to everything we judge. As Maryanne Williams best said: "Everything is Love, or a call for Love." I think its time now more than ever that we are called to learn for ourselves how to ignite our unconditional grace into all that we have judged within ourselves, our world and others.

Thanks again Penny, for saying Yes to birthing this writing and important weaving together. It helps me have greater love and awareness for my soul family on this journey together of coming home."

Past-Life Regression for Soul Healing

Psychologists, psychiatrists, and healers of every stripe have discovered that many of the diseases and disfunctions of this incarnation have their roots in previous ones. Sigmund Freud stated that only by accessing the unconscious, we can learn who we are and with that knowledge, be able to heal. Some people have written that the soul is Freud's unconscious.

We are witnessing a coming together of science, psychology, and spirituality. Hypnosis is the main tool used to help patients access past-life memories. It accesses the wisdom of the subconscious in a focused way to in order to achieve healing. Today there is more acceptance that this is in fact something that can be accessed and healed using tools that were previously regarded as heretical or "woo woo". Thanks to ground-breaking work by acclaimed psychiatrists Brian L Weiss, M.D. and Michael Newton, M.D., hypnosis has moved from a parlor trick to a recognized diagnostic tool for exploring many undiagnosed maladies.

Regression therapy is the mental act of going back to an earlier time, whenever that time may be, in order to retrieve memories that may still be negatively influencing a patient's present life and are probably the source of the patient's symptoms. By revealing the initiatory event that triggered the deviation and possibly progressing them to future life alternatives, they are able to make the course corrections and facilitate healing on a soul level.

Many energy healers are proficient in the field of past-life regression therapy.

Some of the most important revelations of Dr. Brian Weiss's work include:

> *"The soul's primary purpose is to progress towards healing.*
>
> *Just before we die, our soul, that part of us which is aware when it leaves the body, pauses for a moment, floating. In that state it can differentiate color, hear voices, identify objects, and review the life it has just departed. This phenomenon is called an out-of-body experience.*
>
> *Our souls choose our own parents, for our impulse is to continue the learning process so that we can proceed towards healing.*
>
> *We can recognize people from a past lifetime who we know in our current lifetime. Those who are important now were important then and remain with us.*
>
> *Frequently we come back with wounds or weaknesses in the areas of the body that were the site of mortal wounds or damage in a past life.*

People close to starvation, such as those who died in the Holocaust, often become overweight when reincarnated, needing the weight as reassurance they would never be hungry again.

The surest way to be reincarnated into a particular group of people, defined by religion, race, nationality, or culture is to hate those people in a previous life, to be prejudiced or violent against that group.

In regression and progression, symptoms disappear, illnesses get better, and anxiety, depression and fear are relieved.

If you don't change, you're just going to be repeating destructive cycles of aggressor and victim, but if you do change, you can break the cycle.

People often use illness to avoid confronting the issue that lies behind it. Try confronting the illness and asking what it is trying to teach you.

We all have had barbaric lives in the past, suffered the consequences, and have grown from the experience. We should not feel shame or guilt from what we did millennia in the past. We break the cycle through love and compassion.

Those lacking empathy cannot spiritually evolve. Empathy is the key to forgiveness. When we feel a deep emotional identification with younger versions, even past-life manifestations of ourselves, we can appreciate the circumstances that led to our present symptoms and negative judgements.

Empathy heals the individual at the same time it heals the world. It is the sister of compassion and the child of unconditional love.

Compassion is more instinctual, empathy more intellectual.

Usually a child's psychic powers disappear before they reach the age of six.

Atlantis existed forty thousand years ago. They ruled their part of the world because they held the secrets of all matter and all living things. There was a high level of technology that was misused and almost destroyed the planet. People from that time are reincarnating now because our technology is advancing to that level and we have to see if we have learned our lessons. It I the conflict between the compassionate use or selfish use of our advanced power.

In Atlantis physical and mental illness disappeared because people learned how to fix the energetic disruptions that cause disease in the physical dimension.

If we consciously embrace compassion, empathy, love, patience, and forgiveness, the future world will be incredibly different than if we don't. If enough of us can somehow elevate the consciousness of humankind – if we can commit to changing the collective future by improving our individual futures – we can actually change the future of the entire world and its inhabitants.

Meditation and contemplation are handmaidens of patience for they help you achieve distance. As you develop the ability to be quiet, to be introspective and to listen, patience inevitably develops.

Fear closes the mind, love opens the heart and dissolves fear.

Wisdom requires patience. Spiritual growth implies the mastery of patience. Patience allows the unfolding of destiny to proceed at its own unhurried pace.

Violence caused by our own hands and wills, whether toward other humans or against the planet itself, places an individually and the collective in jeopardy. Anger management is a start toward preventing it. People who are violent or suffered violence in past lives frequently have to experience the effects on themselves or others in later lives.

We must heal all our relationships using our core skills of empathy, compassion, nonviolence and love. Communication is the key to every relationship. Love and openness are vital to the process, but so is safety, for if it is not safe to communicate, you won't.

If you can leave a relationship with love, empathy and compassion without any thoughts of revenge, hatred, or fear, that is how you let go.

In future lives you will be together with many of your loved ones, your soul mates, because you are functioning as a family of souls.

If we can laud the strengths of the other and forgive the weaknesses – for they are ours as well – then love will follow.

Real security comes from the knowledge that you are immortal, that you are eternal, and that you can never be harmed.

You can't bring your material things into your next life, but you can bring your deeds, your actions, and your growth – what you have learned and how you are progressing as a spiritual human being. It is also possible that you can take some of your talents.

Self-love is the basis for love of others. It is where real charity begins. Self-love isn't selfish. It is healthy self-esteem.

Contemplation means concentrating on a specific subject or object.

Meditation requires keeping the mind completely blank, in a state of mindfulness or awareness, free to accept whatever feelings, ideas, visions, or images enter it and letting associations flow to all aspects of the object or thought. It is the art of observing without thought, without mental comment.

Meditation chills the chatter that normally fills our mind and the resulting quiet allows us to observe without judgment, to reach a higher level of detachment, and eventually to become of a higher state of consciousness.

Like hypnosis, meditation develops the ability to open the mind to the deepest, most hidden influences on our bodies and souls.

Mindfulness is the awareness of those thoughts, emotions, feelings, and perceptions that are occupying us now, and only now.

Meditation can help us tap into the healing powers within us, not only psychic healing but physical healing as well.

When you come to awareness, you will find yourself compassionate and loving without expecting anything in return. You will feel a oneness with all that is. You will discover your most powerful and essential self.

Love is an absolute quality and energy. It does not stop with our death. It continues on to the other side and returns here again. It is the epitome of the spirit's quality – and the body's. It is life and the afterlife. It is our goal, and all of us, in this or future lives will attain it."

Brian L. Weiss, M.D., Same Soul, Many Bodies

Dr. Brian Weiss has recorded a series of compact discs (CDs) in which he helps you discover and learn techniques of meditation, healing, deep relaxation, and regression.

www.brianweiss.com

By exploring the trajectory of possible paths in future lives, Dr. Weiss helps his patients make conscious choices to align with their soul purpose.

There are many ways besides hypnotherapy regression that people today are "remembering" and connecting with past lives to heal residue energy that is still outstanding, unbalanced, or incomplete. These energies are buried in the subconscious memories and can affect us with programs and discordant energies that tie us to incompletions and traumas of the past that the soul is still learning from.

Thank goodness that we are living in a time where most people not only can utilize a good past-life regressionist to help them heal but many people are "awakening" with memories naturally coming forward for recognition. More and more people are using healing modalities and psychic abilities to access subconscious memories, the Akashic Records, and Higher-Self connections to discern information that can help us heal through the many timelines that still hold the distortions and pain. We can get off karmic wheels of reply in how we treat each other in humanity and utilize the many ways that facilitators can guide us into healing. Soul Retrieval and inner child rescue work are tremendously valuable in helping us reunite with abandoned aspects of ourselves to bring us into wholeness and not bound by trauma of the past.

To access your own past lives...

The more you are able to "get out of your own way" and detach from the outcome, the easier this will be. If you have experience meditating or channeling, or are proficient with kinesiology, muscle testing, or pendulum dowsing, these will be valuable tools in the process but are not necessary.

Find a calm, quiet, safe space where you are unlikely to be interrupted. Have paper and pencil, recording device, or keyboard nearby to record your observations effortlessly.

1. State your intention and what you would like to address or learn about.
2. Go into a meditative state... Breathe deeply... Concentrate on your breath... Visualize a peaceful place where you are an observer of your lives unfolding.
3. Allow this to lead you into a lifetime that has meaning for you. Do not force or make anything happen. This may not be where you think you should be but go with it and let it reveal itself.
4. Begin recording your observations in this Theta state and allow the story to flow effortlessly without censure. Allow the words to flow automatically onto the recording material without thought or scrutiny. This may feel like you are making it up and that is fine. You are able to see details and pick up themes that only you know.
5. What lessons might you learn from this experience that might have application in your present life-expression?
6. Were there any other lifetimes that played on this theme? If so, go there and record what you observe from your soul's vantage point.
7. Does your soul have a message for you in this lifetime?
8. When you are complete, retrace your path back to the present reality.

I find it helpful to reread what I have written several times in order to pick up all of the nuances of what has come through in this altered state. I don't necessarily recall everything that came through, so it is good to have a hard copy. Though it uses my vocabulary, it is quite loving and far more eloquent than I am.

Your soul has a message for you that is found in the notes you have taken from across the veil. If this seems more from the head and not the heart, or If it seems impersonal and lofty, perhaps you were fearful, distracted, protective, or did not go deep enough in order to get past the gatekeeper of the ego. This might take more practice until you are able to tune out the distractions of this incarnation and access the soul messages.

Many of the soul group I asked to participate in this process were amazed at what they came up with, even on their first attempt at "automatic writing". Practice does indeed help.

Reflections on Our Lives Together

In **Dick Sutphen**'s book ***Soul Agreements***, he states:

After 39 years of researching reincarnation and karma, I have come to come conclusions about destiny and the degree to which our earthly path is mapped out. Prior to our birth, while still in spirit, we each decide upon the karma we will confront during our life. Your karmic road map is your astrology chart. Given the date, time, and place of your birth, a talented astrologer can read your life, and by progressing the chart into the present, advise you about the planetary cycles currently affecting you both positively and negatively. Each of us plans our life to experience different degrees of destiny and free will. One person will structure his life plan to include predestined opportunities and to allow very little free will, while another person plans her incarnation to include minimal predestined events and considerable free will. How an incarnation is structured has a lot to do with the kinds of lessons needing to be learned.

I am convinced that even for those who minimize the plausibility of predestined events, major relationships are fated. In other words, we all reincarnated to be together with our parents, lovers, mates, children, and others who affect our lives in the most meaningful ways.

Durga –

The theory of all things: You are a traveling soul. You lived before and experienced former lives. You are the sums of your past experiences, and you are a traveler to the future. Your soul is on a journey to expand, learn, experience. See life as ongoing learning, because it is exactly that. You are well educated. You are a defined character. You prepared yourself very well for this life. Remember your potential. You are your past. We can slow down and collect our memories. A diversity of cultures is your heritage. You are your present. Enjoy the now. Also try to be a better person. Expand who you are. You are your future. Experience the changes and witness the speed of the future. The excitement, the unexpected, the eternal unknowing. We can create things that unveil the inexpressible. Let's get to the good karma. For a long time, I did reincarnation work with people. I always had the ability to see others' former lives that shine through the transparency of today. I have always been most interested in the power that souls have embodied, and how people can bring that power into this life.

Jami

"When I recently reviewed the chart that Penny had made to show many of us in the soul family incarnated at similar times, I experienced so many flash backs at once. Mostly, as if pages were flying off a calendar, I could see the common denominator for my current life. We were all showing up together to come back into alignment with what united us again in common mission. We all seem to be bringing pieces to help ourselves remember a greater story.

We had been so many things to each other for better and for worse. We have fought each other to the death, defended each other and even laid down our life for each other. We have been brothers and sisters, lovers and enemies. We have served, and we have betrayed each other. We have celebrated, and we have mourned. We have felt heaven and we have felt hell with each other. Our journey is taking a delightful turn as we get off the karmic wheel of balancing out "an eye for an eye" behavior and step together once again to join alliance where we were once divided, united again.

I am grateful for all of my experiences that continue to polish me into greater radiance and be able to bring love, compassion, and forgiveness into all areas of my soul path where they are needed. I realize I can only do this by loving everything—including all I may have denied love to, or withheld love from, or been unbalanced with in some way from in my past or parallel timelines. I've had to own and forgive my contributions to the complications I have blamed many antagonists for throughout my life. I believe we all bring many unresolved things forward into our current lives to have new opportunities to heal and balance. Together we can bring old grudges, misalignments and unresolved areas forward into love. Sometimes we both grow into an unconditional love for each other, and sometimes I have to love and allow them to be exactly as they are and forgive myself that I didn't know how to do something better. The point is that I make amends and stop reacting in an old reactionary way and extend love. I don't always get the Disney picture of unconditional love between myself and others because they don't choose it. But I get peace within my being that I no longer cause harm to them with my thoughts, actions, or accusations. In a sense, I can put my sword of righteous down and stop empowering my victims and bring my heart to love for them and to myself for having the courage to extend love and forgive. I am then free for more love and can feel peace and goodness expand within myself.

I see for myself that when I meet someone, if I have an excitement towards meeting them, a nervousness about being in their presence, a sudden desire for them intimately, or a sense of "less than" about myself in their presence, I have work to do. Indeed, something is pulling me into the situation for review. The feelings I have around them intensifies until I do my work to understand what is happening. If I am not conscious of this, I can end up entering some kind of relationship with them that really gets intense, hurtful or even strange as we both are playing out something old and confusing who we are in this timeline from others. Many times, I have entered friendships and family dynamics trying to make up for something I felt I owed them or wanting something I felt they owed me. When I feel this energy, now, I clearly see something is out of balance and it is a call for conscious review and prayerful intention to heal the situation within myself and extend love in the best way I can.

If I don't get the lesson of what's in front of me and bring myself to love, forgiveness and compassionate understanding, I can hold up my evolution. The sooner I have been able to understand why I may be acting or reacting with someone within some situations or involved with them at challenging or highly charged emotional times, the sooner I can be free to be Love and in balance with the people and situations in front of me. Nothing in me then sticks and keeps repeating an old pattern of something old, unforgiven.

A key example of this was I had a love interest friendship with someone that was insistent from the beginning that I marry them. They offered me a financially secure life and adoration. I prayed for the Truth of this kind person in my life and saw that I was married to them in a Middle Eastern lifetime where they died in battle and left me a widow with small children. I was cast aside in that society, as widows were seen as a burden, and lived an awful life. My friend had come to me again thru time and desired to keep me safe and give me what he couldn't before. I saw within the Akashic records that if I married him, and I could have made that choice, I would have spent 17 years with him to realize the same message and lesson I could do now without the marriage contract, and forgive him, love and allow him, and set him free. This way both of us would be free to continue our high evolutionary and transformational lives having the freedom to grow as individually called without entangling the other. This would be a faster evolutionary path for us. I chose this path and gratefully shared my understanding with him. He too then remembered this lifetime that felt incomplete and was relieved to have my forgiveness and blessings for his life. He still wanted the marriage but honored that I needed freedom at this time of my life.

Penny has been and still is a catalyst for me in my recent years to help remember and piece together aspects of myself that more fully remind me of who I am and help me to have better understanding and connection to my Soul Path. I have done this through remembrances of what my meditations show me, what I remember from "activations" within books that I am called to read, by sitting with Penny and other good intuitives that can access the Akashic records and/or access soul records through divinary means by using the oracles or the pendulum, thru a clear channel source such as Penny, and by using my own prayer space to help me access the Sphere of the Akash to help me see with my inner seeing what I am ready to know.

At this point of my evolution, I am able to use my intuition more easily and I can feel and sense and see things more quickly when they are coming to my attention when I meet others. I sit quiet with meditation and prayer and call upon the keepers of the Akash to help me understand. I use muscle testing to confirm, and often sit with Penny to see confirmation thru the pendulum if I need an extra boost of validation. Mostly, I can feel something as true in my heart, because it cracks open with compassion and love and helps me feel the relief of seeing the situation that had me confused or emotional from a "forest above the trees" energy that helps me see and have understanding and love and compassion for all sides. I feel myself relax into love and peace and I can more easily forgive myself and others. I often ask for help from the angels and those of the heavenly realms, along with the Violet Flame and the Fire of Holy Spirit for help in healing and transmuting the energies. I then take whatever action step necessary to share my heart with whomever was involved, which helps me really feel free in the situation. I notice it usually serves their heart as well and clears up any "confusing" or sticky energy between us. I then can take an action step to share my heart with someone that can help me feel really free in the situation, and it usually serves their heart as well and clears up any "confusing" or sticky energy between us.

Thank you for my soul group and to all of us for having the courage and the call to understand the power of traveling with our Soul Group in so many extraordinary ways for learning, loving, and evolving."

Karmas within the Sisterhood:

I have found myself united more and more over the last five years with women who are "temple initiates" through time with me. I often have instant memory/recognition of them when I meet them and often have a sense of which temple or esoteric school we were previously together in. I believe we are finding each other again, crossing paths and "finding" each other again because we are soul family and it is time to reawaken and remember who we really are beyond what we had to forget for whatever reason. It is time, and many of us are getting the call to come together. Our souls are directing us and creating the situations in which we cross paths.

One such experience is my relationship with my Magdalene sisters at our Mary Magdalene Mystery School group in Sedona. (Thanks to Penny Genter) I have always felt a bond with each woman that came into the group. Many of the women I recognized immediately as a "temple sister" with me in previous ancient life times. Often, I would welcome the greeting hug not wanting to let go as we swayed or rocked in a "deep relief" or "celebration" of coming together again. Other times, I would meet a woman I would immediately respect but felt a caution around them, coming from my own being or directed at me from them. I have realized for myself that we have all had loving as well as turbulent life-times together and I was happy to see us come together again to unite, heal and remember that which had been forgotten for many eons thru time. But no matter this knowing, many times I still feel or have felt a "boundary" between us on some level of trust or fully present support and acceptance of each other. It is at these times I have to do my work to clear the "charge" on whatever is coming up for me when I experience hesitation with someone.

I will share a couple examples of my direct experience with my Magdalene sisters. I met a stunning and radiant woman that I instantly admired but felt nervous and "childlike" around her each time I saw her. I felt inadequate and even sometimes guilty around her. I observed my behavior around her for a few months and then I approached her and asked her if I could share something personal with her. She lovingly listened as I told her my experience with myself around her, feeling "nervous" and "inadequate" around her. I asked her forgiveness as I realize with myself that when I feel like this around people I usually have karma with them and owe them an apology, so I apologized for any time in my soul history with her that I had harmed her or been less than grace. This kind and radiant woman lovingly smiled and accepted my apology, sharing that she had no recollection of any incident through time, and then smiled sincerely and told me that I was forgiven no matter what. I felt deep relieved.

As months went on, this woman I had been "nervous" around and I began to share in life experiences and some spiritual work together. At one moment when we were reviewing the Akashic records for many of the women in the Magdalene group, we we're both able to see that we had a life time together as young nuns in a catholic order, somewhere around the age of 12 years old. We enjoyed pranks and laughed a lot together trying to make the best of an intense life style. We often explored mysteries we weren't supposed to within the church and behind closed doors of the institution. My friend got caught and blamed for something I did. Out of my extreme fear of the punishment, I didn't have the chance, or I did not own up to my part in the incident, and my friend was severely and horrifically punished while I was made to watch her suffer. After helplessly watching her suffering for a day, I was then taken away never to see her again. The small amount of joy that I had in that life was taken from me and I died young and lonely with guilt and shame that I was never able to apologize or stand up for my dear friend. After confronting my remorse and the pain of this lifetime, I am appreciative to report that we both smile at our paths crossing again and being able to behold each other in love, grace, kindness, equality and respect. We clearly see the pranksters in each other to this day.

I had also felt a caution with another woman in the Magdalene group that seemed to me to present herself superior in the group. I felt tired or disinterested when she would share. I recently realized that she has been in "superior" positions to me in a couple of life times and ordered my demise. I lost my head under her order in one life time and in another, there was something so hideous that occurred for me that my guidance wouldn't reveal exactly happened. No wonder I was not letting my heart open fully to her. When I realized what it was I was feeling about her, I decided to let her off the hook for being who she was to me in those lifetimes and focus on who she is now as a powerful and paradigm shifting woman of great leadership, I softened my heart to her and decided to own my own contributions to her "wrath" for me in previous life times! I certainly realize that nothing is by coincidence when karmas are involved! This woman played a part for me to experience that was important to my learning on my soul path, and no doubt I didn't always offer the rose to her either.

I have countless situations like this that demonstrate old stuff from previous lifetimes coming up for forgiveness, balance, clearing and transformation. Of the men I have loved, most have been strong alliances from my soul family. This seems to be the lifetime where anything that was out of balance, karmically incomplete, unforgiven or unloved between us shows up for me, up close and personal. I have learned that the stronger the chemistry and attraction, the stronger the karma of something that is incomplete. Chemistry seems to be an unseen force that pulls two people undeniably together. That is my first clue that something is karmic. I don't need to fall in love now every time energy pulls me in attraction. Instead of wondering when I can date the person, I think... uh oh... I better pay attention here. What really does the energy want? And, thankfully, some karma is good karma that comes knocking for new levels of learning, loving and growing together, but that energetic pull is more heart based than intense physical chemistry.

Memories of Being Divided Within the Sisterhood:

In the past five years I have had "flash backs" and memory recall of being in many temples with my temple sisters— from Lemuria to Atlantis to Egypt and Greece and more. I began to recall painful incidents of my past lives where dark forces invaded our priestess and temple spaces. The goal of the invasions was to divide and overpower us. We were turned against each other, implanted to forget what we knew and to mistrust each other. We were often taken as slaves to the dark forces and forced to serve their agendas. If we did not comply our loved ones would be killed. We were forced into what seemed like "damned if we did and damned if we didn't" experiences that created trauma deep within our being. I myself experienced shame in forgetting and feeling like I betrayed my mission and my commitment to bring light and healing to this world. I even remember our Brothers of the Light were turned against us and no longer served to protect us but added to the shame and betrayal we felt. Mistrust was construed in us and amplified over life times to make us forget. The inquisition was a final straw in the agenda of the dark forces to snuff the final fires of the wisdom held deep within women. When my Magdalene sisters began to gather in Sedona, I recognized this trauma in most of the women's energy when I met them. Together, we had experienced the horror and exhaustion of these difficult times, and yet there was so much more...

As we continue to gather, we collectively have more memories of the past come forward.

FAST FORWARD SUMMARY memories with soul family.

Interestingly, my life it seems up until my 48th birthday was fulfilling karma while I was in what I call my level 1 awakening stage of my mission for this lifetime. By my 50th birthday, I had been "called" to Sedona. I took a much-needed sabbatical from over-

responsibilities in life and pursued time to deescalate trauma, drama, and overwhelm in my life. I spent time in nature and rested and laid with my passions for a few months. I need to restore my health from grief and loss exhaustions along with crashed immune, adrenal and nervous system imbalances that demanded time out from my previously "pushing" lifestyle. What I thought would be a little gentle sabbatical began the deepest journey of my life yet. A new phase of my life had begun which I now realize was my next level of awakening. I was now reuniting quickly with the roots of my core soul family confronting, healing, and advancing ourselves in "collective" learning and evolving together.

I have lost count how many times I have moved to different living situations in my 8 years in Sedona. Life there became far more than a sabbatical. It was a call "home" to live, learn, "remember," and, work with my soul alliance team that has incarnated endlessly on this planet. When I met Penny Genter and attended her "Soul Weaving" presentation years ago, I began to see how the dots were connecting. I became attracted to the Magdalene group and anything that Penny was involved with, and it seemed like familiar souls that I knew, and Penny knew kept coming together. People I met had similar passions, pursuits and esoteric experiences. I remember thinking, "where have these people been most of my life? I've missed them!" Often it felt like love at first sight.

The journey I have had with my reuniting with so many people from my soul family has been extraordinary—magical, insightful, nurturing, restorative, evolutionary, revolutionary, and liberating, yet imbued with all of the opposites from those experiences possible. I have had heart-ache, confusions, betrayals, and exhausting emotional upsets as I experienced myself having to offer the rose where perhaps many times in the past I had taken a sword, or the sword had taken me victim. By the sword I mean literally or symbolically, by the sword of my thoughts and actions that were unkind or "less than" in some way. I see for myself that when I come together with soul family, all karmas are due to be balanced, and quickly as we have work to do together and need to "transform" the confusions, misunderstandings and dramas of the past.

Now when I meet members of my soul family, many memories of the past come up naturally. Many things I have forgotten about my greater soul's experience on this planet have been remembered, and peace has been made where there was angst and much fear. The peace that comes with that in my being is extraordinary. Thank you to my soul family for the courage and love that so many of us are committed to bringing forward at this time.

Indeed, together we all learn, live, love and grow. The evolutionary times of late for me have allowed me to "come home" with my soul group to high levels of unconditional love and deep soul remembrance of our history of soul alliance together. My experience is that we are all blossoming ourselves more fully in love, kindness and acceptance. I am so grateful for the soul weaving that my life has experienced with soul family. Again, and again, we seem to show up for each other and travel similar circles of life experiences.

As Ram Dass says, indeed "we are all walking each other home." ...

Penelope Genter, "Penny" (1942-)

Today I am a tapestry of the many threads I bring from all of my previous life experiences. I continue to refine myself to be more reflective of the Divine self, longing for expression. This requires reflection and examination of all aspects of life, past, present, and future which is all one, playing out simultaneously. Still trying to wrap my head around that concept, but I am told it is so. If so, when we heal something in this lifetime, we elevate our experience in all lifetimes and dimensions. Nothing is more important than making all of our experiences exercises in love, for then, now, and always.

One of the "gifts" of advanced years is that we are able to step back and see the patterns in our lives. What are the themes that play out over and over through multiple incarnations? How can we apply love to all of our relationships, especially the "challenging" ones, to "get the message" and move on? Who are our soul mates that show up lifetime after lifetime to assist us on the path? These answers are hidden just beneath the surface of our lives if we are able to detach from the emotion of the moment and look closer at the patterns of our lives together.

We all have experienced many opportunities for growth and awareness through our many incarnations. Each "ah ha" moment allows us to step higher up the ladder, so we do not have to experience that trauma again. The more we let go of the ego, the easier it becomes.

I am grateful for all of my experiences, even the painful ones, for they allowed me to work through my karma and receive the grace of understanding. I am grateful for all my soul mates who have assisted me on this journey, especially when it was difficult. I do believe that this is a group process and we are our brother's/sister's keeper in that we hold the keys to understanding and growth creating the tapestry of life. We are all holding hands on the journey home...

Namaste,

Penny

About the author

Penelope Genter has spent a lifetime studying the face of God and how this is mirrored in all of our relationships. She outlived three husbands and has ten children and stepchildren, fifteen grandchildren, and five great-grandchildren. She is an accomplished dowser, Master Gardener, and had her own design business for over 30 years. She produced and marketed flower and gem essences, taught at university and at numerous workshops and seminars. She is a Unity of Sedona Chaplain and facilitated the Mary Magdalene Circle there for five years. She taught the 16 week *Creating Sacred Relationships Class* at Unity in early 2015 based upon Mother Mary's teachings she channeled. She facilitated a Sophia Woman's group in Sedona from 2015-2017. She now facilitates a Magdalene Mystery School in Sedona, AZ.

In 2015 Penny was one of the presenters in the Premier GODTALKS™ presentation in Sedona, AZ. This is available on YouTube and at www.godtalkssedona.com . YouTube also has her talk on **Searching for Mary Magdalene**.

Penelope has written other books with Mother Mary and her partners in spirit that are meant to inspire people to see their own inner divinity and to share this loving awareness with others on the path.

Other books by Penelope/Penny Genter

Touching Home—Roadmaps for the New Age (E-book) 1998

Returning Home—A Workbook for Ascension 2001

2013 Blueprints for the New Paradigm (E-book) 2007

Hieros Gamos – The Sacred Union of the Divine Feminine and Divine Masculine available on Amazon and Kindle.2016

Sar'h – A story of Tamar, Firstborn of Mary Magdalene and Jesus the Christ, for those with ears to hear available on Amazon, Kindle and Audible. 2017

The Messenger – Healing Breast Cancer. Following a healing path through Eastern and Western Medicine with Angelic Guidance. Available on Amazon and Kindle. 2018

Index

Glossary

Akashic Records are a compendium of all human events, thoughts, words, emotions, and intent ever to have occurred in the past, present, or future. They are believed by theosophists to be encoded in a non-physical plane of existence known as the etheric plane. Our Akashic records are found in our DNA,

Council of Nicaea - Emperor Constentine "The Great" called the First Council of Nicaea in 325AD, at which the Nicene Creed was adopted by Christians. The dating of Easter was established. Rules were framed that defined the authority of bishops, thereby paving the way for a concentration of power in ecclesiastical hands.

They decided by vote that Jesus was a god, not a mortal prophet, thus merging conveniently with Sol Invictus, the sun god.

A year after the Council of Nicaea, Constentine sanctioned the confiscation and destruction of all works that challenged orthodox teachings, works by pagan authors that referred to Jesus, as well as works by "heretical" Christians.

He also arranged for a fixed income to be allocated to the Church and installed the bishop of Rome (Pope) in the Lateran Palace.

In 331AD he commissioned and financed new copies of the Bible. In 303AD, a quarter century earlier, the pagan emperor Diocletian had undertaken to destroy all Christian writings that could be found. This enabled the custodians of orthodoxy to revise, edit, and rewrite their material as they saw fit in accordance with their tenants.

Channeling usually refers to accessing higher knowledge in order to support spiritual growth and to gain greater clarity about one's life. Channeling is a means of communicating with any consciousness that is not in human form by allowing that consciousness to express itself through the channel (or channeler). We live in a multidimensional universe. The physical plane is only the first (and most dense) of seven planes. The next plane is the astral; we dwell on the lower astral plane before birth and after death. The other planes are the causal, akashic, mental, messianic, and buddhaic. Through channeling, we can make conscious contact with higher planes. We can also communicate with beings who are physical but nonhuman, such as devas (nature spirits), dolphins and whales, and extraterrestrials.

Edgar Cayce March 18, 1877 – January 3, 1945) was an American clairvoyant who answered questions on subjects as varied as healing, reincarnation, wars, Atlantis, and future events while claiming to be in a trance. A biographer gave him the nickname, "The Sleeping Prophet". A nonprofit organization, the Association for Research and Enlightenment was founded to facilitate the study of Cayce's work.

Download When I say I "download" something, it is similar to receiving something on a computer – I intuitively channel or receive information and record it on my computer without censoring it.

"**Get"** For the purpose of this book, when I say I "get" something it means that I have received a message intuitively and have verified it with kinesiology or muscle testing.

Karma The word *karma* is a Sanskrit term that means "work, deed, or act"; it has also been interpreted to mean "cause and effect." Perhaps one of the most intriguing and unique philosophical contributions is the idea that *karma can simply be defined as memory.* It is a pool of information that the subconscious mind draws upon and can utilize in the present. It has elements that are positive as well as those which seem negative.

Kinesiology – or muscle testing is a form of energy dowsing that uses the energy systems body as a "lie detector" to give either positive or negative feedback. This can be used to test for physical conditions, health, disease, or to calibrate truth on a numeric scale as described by Dr. David Hawkins in his book ***Power vs. Force***.

Mediumship - The most common form of communication with nonphysical consciousness is with people who have passed on, but that is usually referred to as "mediumship" rather than channeling. A medium, as defined here, might also provide this kind of information, but the intent in seeing a medium is usually to communicate with a specific person who has passed on who would not necessarily be expert in accessing such information. Although those on the astral plane are generally more objective about physical experience than we are here on the physical plane, being nonphysical doesn't automatically make someone skillful, knowledgeable, wise, or loving; every consciousness must earn its "enlightenment."

Monad In some gnostic systems the Supreme Being is known as the **Monad**, the One, the Absolute, the creative principle of all things.

Predictions. Since the future, by definition, hasn't happened yet, it is impossible to make consistently accurate predictions. Some psychics and channeled sources are adept at picking up probabilities based on where things are heading, but since each individual has free will--probabilities are constantly shifting as we make choices--nobody knows for sure. Even when certain changes are more or less inevitable, the form they take, and the way people react to them are not. Timing is especially difficult to predict. Rather than asking if and when an event will happen, it might be more useful to ask what percentage the probability is, and if there are agreements or karmas putting force behind its happening.

Reincarnation It is the recycling of souls until perfection of the spirit is achieved and reunification with the God spirit occurs. Edgar Cayce preferred to call it, "The Continuity of Life."

Trance Channel a person who is able to set their conscious self aside in order to allow another being, a non-physical or spirit being, to speak through their body. The person who does this is the channel. They are unaware of the information that comes through or what transpires in the session. The being who does the speaking is usually referred to as an entity or spirit guides. Channels, as we use the term, usually will allow more highly evolved beings and spirit teachers to come through and speak. The more highly evolved entities do not usually engage in psychic demonstrations if they are for entertainment purposes only. They are much more interested in helping us learn and grow personally and as a people. With trance channeling, the channel more fully steps aside and allows the entity full and direct control over all speaking and physical movement. The voice used by the entity to speak through the channel is usually distinctly different from the channel's "normal" voice. The facial movements and other physical mannerisms are also distinctly different in trance channeling. In many respects, when you speak to an entity who is being trance channeled, you are speaking directly to that entity without the channel's personality acting as an intermediary or translator. The experience is like having an interactive conversation with a very wise, very loving person. Each entity has its own distinctive personality. Upon returning, the channel is unaware of the "conversation" that has taken place.

Bibliography

Karma and Reincarnation

Edgar Cayce on the Akashic Records: The Book of Life, 1997

Kevin J. Todeschi: author

Karma and Reincarnation: The Wisdom of Yogananda, 2007

by Paramhansa Yogananda

Journey of Souls: Case Studies of Life Between Lives, 1994

by Michael Newton (Author)

Life Between Lives: Hypnotherapy for Spiritual Regression, 2004

by Michael Newton (Author)

Destiny of Souls: New Case Studies of Life Between Lives, 2000

by Michael Newton (Author)

Many Lives, Many Masters: The True Story of a Prominent Psychiatrist, His Young Patient, and the Past-Life Therapy That Changed Both Their Lives, 1988 by Brian L. Weiss

Miracles Happen: The Transformational Healing Power of Past-Life Memories, 2013

by Brian L. Weiss and Amy E. Weiss

Same Soul, Many Bodies: Discover the Healing Power of Future Lives through Progression Therapy, 2005

by Brian L. Weiss M.D. (Author)

Soul Agreements, 2005, Dick Sutphen and Tara Sutphen

You Were Born Again to be Together, 1976, Dick Sutphen

Past Lives, Future loves, 1987, Dick Sutphen

Kinesiology and Energy Dowsing

Behaving as If the God in All Life Mattered, 1997

by Machaelle Small Wright

Perelandra Garden Workbook: A Complete Guide to Gardening with Nature Intelligences, 1993

by Machaelle Small Wright

Flower Essences: Reordering Our Understanding and Approach to Illness and Health, 1988

by Machaelle Small Wright

Power vs. Force, 2014

by David R. Hawkins M.D. Ph.D.

Lemuria, Atlantis & Ramtha

The Story of Atlantis and the Lost Lemuria, 2016

by W. Scott Elliot

Edgar Cayce's Atlantis and Lemuria: The Lost Civilizations in the Light of Modern Discoveries , 2001

by Frank Joseph

Ramtha: The White Book, 1986

by Ramtha and J. Z. Knight

Egypt

Akhenaten: The Heretic Pharaoh, 2016

by Brien Foerster

Akhenaten and the Origins of Monotheism, 2015

by James K. Hoffmeier

RETURN OF THE GODDESS: The Hidden History of Nefertiti - Akhenaten - Mary Magdalene - Scotia, 2015

By Jeri Castronova

CLEOPATRA: THE EGYPTIAN QUEEN: THE ENTIRE LIFE STORY, 2018

by THE HISTORY HOUR

Jesus and the Essenes

***The Aquarian Gospel of Jesus the Christ*: The Philosophic and Practical Basis of the Religion of the Aquarian Age of the World and of the Church**, 1982 by Levi

The Way of the Essenes: Christ's Hidden Life Remembered, 1992

by Anne Meurois-Givaudan, Daniel Meurois-Givaudan

Anna, the Voice of the Magdalenes, 2010

by Claire Heartsong and Catherine Ann Clemett

Anna, Grandmother of Jesus: A Message of Wisdom and Love, 2017

by Claire Heartsong

Jesus The Book, 2009

by Durga Holzhauser and Frank Eickermann

***Jesus the forgotten Years* (The series of the sacred stories) (Volume 2)** 2018

by Durga Holzhauser and Agni F. Eickermann

***The Holy Women Around Jesus*, 2005**

by Carol Haenni, Edgar Cayce, Sister Ann Catherine Emerick

Bloodline of the Holy Grail: The Hidden Lineage of Jesus Revealed, 2002

by Laurence Gardner

Jesus after the Crucifixion: From Jerusalem to Rennes-le-Château, 2007

by Graham Simmans

Rex Deus: The True Mystery of Rennes-Le-Chateau and the Dynasty of Jesus, 2000

By Marilyn Hopkins, Tim Wallace-Murphy, Graham Simmans

Custodians of Truth: The Continuance of Rex Deus, 2005

by Tim Wallace-Murphy, Marilyn Hopkins

The Way of the Essenes: Christ's Hidden Life Remembered, 1992

by Anne Meurois-Givaudan, Daniel Meurois-Givaudan

The Complete Works of Flavius Josephus - Legendary Jewish Historian and His Chronicle of Ancient History, 2008 by translation by William Whiston

Montsegur and the Mystery of the Cathars, 2003

by Jean Markale

The Treasure of Montsegur: A Novel of the Cathars, 2003

by Sophy Burnham

The Knights of the Holy Grail: The Secret History of The Knights Templar, 2016

by Tim Wallace-Murphy

The Knights Templar: The Hidden History of the Knights Templar: The Church's Oldest Conspiracy, 2015

by Conrad Bauer

The Templars: The History and the Myth: From Solomon's Temple to the Freemasons, 2009

by Michael Haag

Personal Recollections of Joan of Arc,

by Mark Twain

The Other Boleyn Girl, 2002

by Philippa Gregory

Mozart: The Man Revealed, 2017

by John Suchet

The House of Medici: Its Rise and Fall, 1999

by Christopher Hibbert

The Poet Prince: A Novel (The Magdalene Line), 2010

by Kathleen McGowan

The Medici: Godfathers of the Renaissance, 2009

by Paul Strathern

A Sketch of the Life and Public Services of James Mitchell Varnum of Rhode Island (Classic Reprint) 2018

by James Mitchell Varnum

The Impressionists

The Judgment of Paris: The Revolutionary Decade That Gave the World Impressionism, 2006

by Ross King

Occult Paris: The Lost Magic of the Belle Époque, 2016

by Tobias Churton

The Invisible History of the Rosicrucians: The World's Most Mysterious Secret Society, 2009

by Tobias Churton

The Private Lives of the Impressionists, 2006

By Sue Roe

Luncheon of the Boating Party, 2008

by Susan Vreeland